# How to be the HAPPY WIFE of an Unsaved Husband

## Linda Davis

Whitaker House

PITTSBURGH & COLFAX STREETS, SPRINGDALE, PA. 15144

Scripture quotations marked (NAS) are taken from the *New American Standard Bible*, © The Lockman Foundation, 1960, 1962, 1963, 1968, 1971, 1972, 1973, 1975, 1977, and used by permission.

Quotations from *The Mustard Seed Conspiracy*, by Tom Sine, copyright © 1981, are used by permission of Word Books, Waco, Texas 76796.

# HOW TO BE THE HAPPY WIFE OF AN UNSAVED HUSBAND

Linda Davis
Sparrow's Nest Ministries
P.O. Box 973
Chesterfield, MO 63017

ISBN: 0-88368-189-7
Printed in the United States of America
Copyright © 1987 by Linda Davis

Whitaker House
580 Pittsburgh Street
Springdale, PA 15144

# CONTENTS

## DEDICATION

This book is dedicated to Mark—my Love, my Joy, and my Christian husband worth the wait—and to our sons, Scot and Todd, with appreciation for their role in bringing their father to the Lord.

# FOREWORD

In a tactful and personal way, Linda Davis confronts the delicate and sometimes difficult issues raised when a believing woman is married to an unbelieving husband. Although the book is primarily addressed to women in this unique situation, much of what the author has to say would be helpful to any married woman. *How To Be The Happy Wife Of An Unsaved Husband* will be an excellent tool for women's ministry, as well as a textbook for adult Christian education.

From a strong biblical perspective, the spiritual issues at war over the control of a marriage are forthrightly addressed. And the man's point of view is surprisingly well-represented in this practical primer on how to survive and get the most out of marriage when your spouse is not a believer.

Dr. Richard Dobbins
Director, Emerge Ministries, Inc.

# INTRODUCTION

The first time I showed the manuscript for this book to Donna Arthur of Whitaker House, she asked me, "Why do you feel that the Lord called you to write this book?"

That question took me by surprise. I knew I had written it in response to a definite prompting—a divine burden in fact. I would rather have written about a simpler topic, but whenever I wasn't writing I felt as guilty as a child shirking her homework. When I could bear the guilt no longer, I would sit down and write another chapter.

But *why me*? There must be hundreds of women yearly whose husbands get saved after years of resistance. There are no doubt more pious Christians and much better scholars of His Word than I. Certainly there are better and more experienced writers than this novice.

So my only reply to Donna's question was an honest, "I don't know. I guess nobody else would do it."

But, upon reflection, a familiar scripture leaped out at me, and I knew I had the answer. I saw myself described in 1 Corinthians 1:27-29:

> "God has chosen the foolish things of the world to shame the wise, and God has chosen the weak things of the world to shame the things which are strong, and the base things of the world and the despised, God has chosen . . . that no man should boast before God."

While acknowledging my own unworthiness—my foolishness and weakness—to write this volume, I saw that it was for those very reasons that God chose me to do it.

I believe God has seen fit to choose from their own ranks one to speak for those who live "quiet lives of desperation" in the Body of Christ. He wants to offer a kind word to those starving for appreciation for their monumental task of serving both Christ and a husband who rejects Him.

God has chosen to tell these women that, yes, they may be foolish, weak, and even despised. But it is through their inadequacies that He can be adequate. Through their acceptance of themselves as imperfect and incapable of doing what only God can do, they can be healed of their unnecessary guilt. And through their faithfulness He can win even the most stubborn heart to Christ.

That, I pray, is the message of this book.

# 1

# DON'T BLAME
# YOURSELF

*"There is therefore now no condemnation for
those who are in Christ Jesus"*—Romans 8:1.

Do you believe the above verse, or are you
secretly blaming yourself because your husband
isn't yet a Christian? How often do you catch yourself thinking, If only I were doing certain things
better—loving, submitting, witnessing—he would
already be a born-again wonder? Do you ever feel
like he won't accept Christ because your failures
and imperfections are a stumbling block: If I hadn't
been so crabby the other day? If I weren't always
yelling at the kids? If I hadn't run up the charge
account? Do you ever blame yourself?

Then I have good news for you: *it isn't your
fault!* You may never have heard anyone say that
before. No one ever said it to me. In fact, everyone seemed to be saying just the opposite. Not out-
right, of course. That wouldn't be polite. They
didn't walk up to my face and say, "It's all your

9

fault that your husband isn't a Christian. If you would just obey the Bible and take my advice, your husband would get saved right away." No, they were a *little* more subtle in heaping on the guilt. They said things like:

"If you ladies with unsaved husbands would just be more sweet and loving, your husbands would get born-again in *no time."* (This direct quote came from a retreat leader whose husband had been a Christian since age six.)

"As soon as the Lord finishes working on *you,* then He will start working on your husband." (Can't He work on both of us at the same time?)

"Why don't you try being a Total Woman?" (What am I now, half man?)

"Just pray longer." (Fifteen years isn't long enough?)

"You just need to love your husband to the Lord." (What do you think I'm doing, scrubbing the toilet with his toothbrush?)

I'm sure you can supply dozens of other pat remarks made by well-intentioned Christians— from the pulpit to the pew. They are usually pontificated by folks who have no idea what you are going through or how complex the situation can be. The jabs that hurt the most are the pieces of glib advice coming from a woman whose husband *did* get saved after they were married and who proudly takes all the credit. She never stops to think that things might not have been so easy were she married to *your* husband—or that her husband might have gotten saved in half the time if he had been married to you.

## The Weight Of Guilt

All resentment aside, much of that glib advice may very well be true and good as far as it goes (it's never all that simple.) But after a while I began to wonder why every time I admitted, "My husband isn't a Christian," someone started pointing a finger at me. It made me feel like I had some very obvious flaws—everyone else could immediately point them out.

Such advice, piling up over the years, finally placed me under so much condemnation that I dreaded walking into church alone. I felt that my mere solitary presence flashed, "Failure! Failure! Failure!" in neon lights. At one point I came close to dropping out of church altogether, which would have been disastrous.

Christians who are quick to point out what you should be doing differently may be suffering from the delusion that they have all the answers. After all, *their* mate is saved; whatever worked for them will surely work for you. What they fail to realize is that no one can lead another person to Christ if his heart is not ready to surrender. Every man has his own set of barriers and misconceptions, as well as his own history of hurts and fears. And the Holy Spirit is not a computer into which you

11

can push the correct formula to obtain the proper programmed responses. He is wise, sensitive, and patient enough to treat each and every person as an individual.

When the church blames the wives of unbelievers, it may be out of guilt for not being able to do more. The sad truth is that no one is to blame. Your husband's relationship with God is strictly up to him. God has given him a free will that neither you nor the church can manipulate with techniques. You cannot force him, trick him, or bribe him into getting saved before he is ready. God won't violate your husband's free will, and He won't let you, either.

Of course you should be as loving, devoted, and biblically submissive as you can be. But the plain truth is that your being the world's most perfect, submitted wife does *not* guarantee that your husband will ever become a Christian. He may get saved tomorrow, or it may take fifty years for the Lord to break through his hardened heart. That is not why we are loving, devoted, and submissive—we do it all simply because that is the way the Lord wants us to be, period. No ulterior motives. No payoff. Just obedience.

But whether your husband gets saved today or fifty years from now is no reflection on you. Just because he is not yet saved does not mean that you are any less of a wife and Christian than the woman whose husband got saved twenty years ago. It takes more than a perfect wife to save a husband. Men get saved without perfect wives. God must save your husband. You can certainly be helpful, but not by thinking it is your job.

On judgment day your husband will not be allowed to use you as an excuse for being an unbeliever. "But, Lord, this woman you gave me . . . " didn't work for Adam, and it won't work for your husband, either. You can give your husband what he thinks are excellent excuses for not being a Christian by acting in an unbecoming manner. But if he really wanted to know the Lord, I doubt you could stop him.

So isn't it silly to think that your imperfections could stop your husband from getting saved if he were ready? How many men do you know who got saved because their wives were perfect? I don't know any. In fact, some of the most nearly perfect wives I know have the most gospel-resistant husbands. And some of the most self-centered women I know have the most dear, Christian husbands. Who can explain it? To me it's just more proof that a man's relationship with God depends more on his own heart than his wife's.

## Loosing Your Husband To God

A woman should seek to please her husband more for God's sake than for the ulterior motive of getting her husband saved. God's will is to save your husband, regardless of your state of perfection. It may not happen as soon as you would like, but it will happen as soon as heavenly possible. The Lord wants you to seek Him, trust Him, and obey Him with all your heart just because you love Him—not out of guilt. Satan, not God, is the "accuser of the brethren."

Not only can you let go of all that guilt, but you *must*, for your sake and your husband's. In Matthew 16:19, Jesus said,

> "I will give you the keys of the kingdom of heaven; and whatever you shall bind on earth shall be bound in heaven, and whatever you shall loose on earth shall be loosed in heaven."

When you carry around worry and guilt over your husband's spiritual condition, you are actually "binding" him. Each negative thought is like another cord wrapped tightly around his heart, making it harder for the Holy Spirit to get in there and soften it up. This spiritual principle works— release him completely to the Lord, relax, and watch the Holy Spirit take over.

Worry and guilt also bind you. But when you accept *God's* acceptance of you just the way you are and trust that He will save your husband at the earliest possible moment, you cut away those constricting cords of guilt and worry and allow yourself to grow spiritually, too. Then you are free to begin anew, being the best wife you can be, not out of guilt but for the sheer joy of it.

# 2

# DON'T BLAME GOD

*"The Lord is not slow about His promise, as some count slowness, but is patient toward you, not wishing for any to perish but for all to come to repentance"*—2 Peter 3:9.

Have you ever gotten angry with God because your husband isn't saved? You pray and pray for his salvation as the weeks, months, and years go by. You search the Bible for scriptures to cling to—verses that give you hope to keep on believing despite circumstances. You recite them, commit them to memory, and claim them boldly.

You do all you can to be a model wife—submit to your husband in all things, keep yourself as attractive as possible, and act lovingly toward your husband even when he may not be acting the same way back to you.

Time and again you forgive him for hurting your feelings or letting you down. He promises to go to church but doesn't go after all, making a flimsy excuse at the last minute. Or he goes and sits there like a rock, angry because he "got talked into it." Perhaps he seems to enjoy it, but nothing happens. The gospel affects him about as much as yesterday's newspaper.

Every time you get your hopes up they come crashing down, shattering like broken promises. Your balancing act has failed again, and you crumble under the weight of your own disappointment. Despairing, you cry out to God, "Why don't You *do* something? Can't you see this is killing me? I need Your help! Will You *ever* save my husband?"

Then you cry and refuse to speak to God for at least two days because, after all, He isn't listening. He is too busy running the universe to listen to your insignificant prayers. "Other women's husbands are getting saved all over the place," you complain. "What are they doing right that I'm not? Why does God listen to their prayers and not mine? I must not matter at all." And your mood becomes blacker still.

Have you ever been through this scenario? How did I guess? I was there many times myself in the fifteen years that I waited for my husband to become a Christian.

### God's Perfect Timing

Eventually I came to understand how foolish it was to blame God because my husband wasn't saved. I began to realize, "Was it not the Lord who suffered and died on the cross for my husband? And here I am complaining when I have not come close to suffering to that extent. The Lord wants my husband's salvation much more than I do. Hasn't He proved that already?''

I also began to understand that my motives were not entirely pure and unselfish. My longing for his salvation had much to do with my desire for my own happiness. But God's motives for wanting him saved came from only one thing: agape love—love that gives with no strings attached. He desires that your husband be saved for your husband's sake alone. God's timing is set accordingly, for the moment your husband will be most ready to believe.

It grieves the Father for us to think that He would hold out on us. That was what Eve thought when she bit into the forbidden fruit. The Bible promises that our Father is not a withholder but a Giver of good and perfect gifts.

> "If you then, being evil, know how to give good gifts to your children, how much more shall your Father who is in heaven give what is good to those who ask Him!"—Matthew 7:11.
>
> "Every good thing bestowed and every perfect gift is from above, coming down from the Father of lights, with whom there is no variation, or shifting shadow"—James 1:17.

No, it is not God's fault that your husband is not saved. He is not withholding so you will become a better person or learn through suffering, as many people think. God wants your husband saved as soon as possible so He can begin to shower him with good and perfect gifts. If living with your husband until he becomes a Christian makes you more Christlike, as it most likely will and already has, that's just icing on the cake. But that won't keep you from continuing to become a better person after he is saved. Your becoming a better person is secondary to your husband's salvation on God's priority list.

## The True Culprit

If your husband's spiritual condition isn't God's fault, whose is it? The answer is found in John 10:10. "The thief comes only to steal, and kill, and destroy; I came that they might have life, and might have it abundantly." This thief is the same one that Jesus spoke of in Matthew 13:19, "When anyone hears the word of the Kingdom, and does not understand it, the evil one comes and snatches away what has been sown in his heart."

Now you see who the culprit really is—that old Word-snatcher, the devil. He should be the object of your anger. Go ahead and get angry! Get real mad at the devil! He is responsible for both your husband's unbelief and your despair.

The next time that "old serpent" tempts you to despair, do something that will make him writhe. Quote Scripture just like Jesus did when He was tempted. Shout out loud, "I will wait for the Lord, I will be strong and let my heart take courage." (See Psalm 27:14.) "I will bless the Lord at all times; His praise shall continually be in my mouth" (Psalm 34:1). Repeat those verses over and over until they are bubbling up in your spirit and you really believe them.

Then you can pull out your personal checkbook and write a nice donation to your favorite ministry. Wave it in Satan's face and say, "Here, you old snake, this one's on you! This check will be used to spread the gospel and feed the poor. And I'll write another one, in your honor, if you try to tempt me to despair again."

Another way of defeating Satan is to make your husband's favorite special dinner. Surprise him at the door with a big kiss, your best perfume, soft music, and candlelight. Be sure to tell the devil you're glad the temptation he sent you made you think of doing such a nice thing for your husband. Next time he'll think twice before pulling out his old bag of tricks.

James 4:7 says, "Resist the devil and he will flee from you." He truly will.

Being on the offensive against the devil is far better than being on the defensive—you can't win a war without launching an attack. Resisting Satan doesn't mean hanging on by your fingernails.

It means putting on your spiritual "armor" and going after him. (See Ephesians 6:10-17.) Rout the enemy, and chase him off! Both you and the devil know that he cannot stand against the name of Jesus Christ when it is wielded by a believer.

The only way Satan can win is to get you mad at the only One who is truly on your side. So remember who the real enemy is, and remember who the real King of kings is. Together you'll make a great winning combination. You and Jesus can't be beat!

# 3
# CHRIST'S AMBASSADOR

*"Therefore, we are ambassadors for Christ, as though God were entreating through us; we beg you on behalf of Christ, be reconciled to God"*—2 Corinthians 5:20.

The Christian wife of an unsaved husband has a special ministry that no one else has. Corrie Ten Boom touched thousands, and Sandi Patti ministers to multitudes with her singing; but only you can be Christ's ambassador in your home.

When you made Christ your Savior and Lord, the Holy Spirit literally came to dwell within you. Jesus said, "If anyone loves Me, he will keep My word; and My Father will love him, and We will come to him, and make Our abode with him" (John 14:23). Do you realize how special that makes you? Do you realize that wherever you go, Jesus goes? Whenever you walk into a room, the people in that room are blessed because you have brought Christ into their midst.

you know that your husband, even though he is an unbeliever, is sanctified—set apart for holy use—through you? 1 Corinthians 7:14 says,

> For the unbelieving husband is sanctified through his wife, and the unbelieving wife is sanctified through her believing husband; for otherwise your children are unclean, but now they are holy.

Doesn't that make you feel good?

The world is under the control of Satan. God created man to have dominion over the earth, but when man fell into sin he forfeited that dominion to Satan, "the prince of the power of the air" (Ephesians 2:2). Jesus came to earth to re-establish His Kingdom within us—that was the good news He preached. "Behold, the kingdom of God is within you" (Luke 17:21 *KJV*). All who have been born again are free of Satan's control and are ambassadors of God's Kingdom on the earth.

## The King's Representative

If, as 2 Corinthians 5:20 says, we are ambassadors for Christ, how should we act?

When an American ambassador visits a foreign country, he walks with all the dignity and authority that is due his title. His clothes are impeccable, and his buttons shine. Standing erect, he conducts himself like royalty, not because he personally is so important but because his nation is.

It would never do to have an insecure, shoddy weakling representing the American government. What a disgrace that would be. A mighty nation deserves a representative of the same caliber.

That is why we, as representatives of the mighty King of kings, should never hang our heads apologetically. We must not disgrace the One we are to represent by being any less than the best we can be. We must walk with all the dignity and confidence that belongs to us in Christ. The world and your husband may still be under the headship of the Impostor, but you are not. Let them clearly see the difference between you and the world.

Before I knew Christ I was in sad shape. I looked like Poor Pitiful Pearl. Pale and frail, my shoulders were always stooped. My wardrobe did nothing for me, yet I felt unworthy to spend money on myself for clothes. I was shy and insecure, but I tried to cover that up with loudness at times. Sure that I would fail, I never tried to accomplish anything. My self-esteem depended entirely upon what my husband and others thought of me from day to day. Life was a roller coaster of ups and downs—mostly downs.

Then along came Jesus! He looked me right in the eye and said, "Linda, I love you. You are beautiful."

And I believed Him.

Today there is a new me. Every morning I take a fragrant bath, put on my makeup, and dress myself in something attractive because I think Jesus deserves a pretty ambassador. Every day is a joy. I have confidence, not because of *who* I am but because of *Whose* I am.

When my children started school, I went to college and became a registered nurse. A few years later I took my real estate license exam and became a member of the Million Dollar Club within my first year as an agent. Right now I am learning to fly hot air balloons. And I am writing this book, expecting that the Lord will use it to bless you and glorify Himself.

The more I mature, the gutsier I get. I have learned from past experience that whatever the Lord gives me to do, He will help me to do well. Jesus wants successful ambassadors.

I expect people to like me, and they usually do. If they don't, at least Jesus thinks I'm terrific!

### Learning To Blossom

In letting your life show the difference between the world and God's Kingdom, you may be surprised how many people notice. Your husband will notice, too. I won't promise that by behaving like Christ's ambassador in your home your husband will instantly become a convert. Only God can save souls. But a little favorable influence can surely pave the way.

I *can* promise, however, that you will enjoy your life more and like yourself much better if you base your self-esteem upon who you are in Christ. And you can't help but win your husband's admiration when he sees the real you blossoming. God put a truly beautiful person in there. Don't let poor self-esteem or false teaching about "humility" hide that beauty. Many women have been taught that wearing makeup and looking attractive are of the devil. Satan must love it when Christian women look anything but their best. We owe it to the Lord to let all that beauty out!

"That sounds great," you say, "but how do I do that? How can I achieve my greatest potential?"

First, you must believe in yourself. It may be a cliche, but it's true that "God doesn't make junk." God makes beautiful, wondrous things, but people take those things and make junk out of them. Have you been allowing people to make junk out of you? Do you believe all the negative things the world tells you about yourself?

"You're just plain lazy." "If only you were more like your sister." "You need a higher I.Q. to think about doing that." "Your nose is too big." The world just can't wait to tell you the bad news.

That is why Jesus came with the good news: "The kingdom of God is within you"; "If any man is in Christ, he is a new creature; the old things passed away; behold, new things have come"; and, "You are the light of the world" (Luke 17:21; 2 Corinthians 5:17; Matthew 5:14).

How's that for starters? And there is much more in God's Word if you will just believe Him. When doing your daily Bible reading, use a highlighter to mark all the verses that promise what a wonderful person you are—and are becoming—in Christ!

If you feel that you aren't quite there yet, don't give up. Even Paul said of himself,

> Brethren, I do not regard myself as having laid hold of it yet; but one thing I do: forgetting what lies behind and reaching forward to what lies ahead, I press on toward the goal for the prize of the upward call of God in Christ Jesus—Philippians 3:13-14.

If the Bible says that you are being "conformed to the image of His Son" (Romans 8:29), then you *are*. God can't lie. Being a Christian means walking in faith—faith not only in God but in *God in you*. So believe in yourself.

Secondly, keep yourself as attractive as possible. Sounds worldly? I think not. Esther, in the Old Testament, didn't think so, either. She spent a lot of time making herself attractive—"six months with oil of myrrh and six months with spices and the cosmetics for women" (Esther 2:12)—so God could use her for His purposes. Sarah, Abraham's wife, was so beautiful that even in her old age younger men desired her. (See Genesis 20.) My favorite role model, the godly woman of Proverbs 31, wore "fine linen and purple" (verse 22).

It only makes sense that God's women should be the most beautiful women on earth. We have God's wisdom to teach us what looks most becoming. We have God's modesty to keep us from looking cheap or gaudy. We have God's self-control to eat properly for good health and proper weight control. And we have God's Holy Spirit within us to make us glow from the inside out.

> Let not your adornment be external only—braiding the hair, and wearing gold jewelry, or putting on dresses; but let it be the hidden person of the heart, with the imperishable quality of a gentle and quiet spirit, which is precious in the sight of God—1 Peter 3:3-4.

Wow! Even Hollywood movie stars can't compete with that kind of beauty. Theirs is merely "external," but we Christian women can have both internal *and* external beauty. What an advantage. Our beauty both makes us look good and is a direct compliment to the Lord and our husbands.

### Practical Steps To Success

To learn how best to beautify yourself, go to the experts for advice. Buy or check out of the library some good books on how to dress according to your body dimensions and your lifestyle. It is a shame for a woman to be ignorant of a few simple facts. Any good grooming book contains countless tips to help you look your best.

Also, try to keep up with the times. You need not be a slave to every new fad that comes around, but it is just as bad to look exactly like you did when you graduated from high school twenty years ago. Face it, stiff teased hair and the Cleopatra look are dead!

Then invest in what I believe is one of the best things a woman can do for herself—a color analysis. Let a color consultant show you what colors, in clothes and make-up, look most becoming on you. You will be buying new clothes for the rest of your life, so why not get them in the colors that are most flattering to you? You will have the added bonus of saving money on clothes, makeup, and accessories. When they are all color co-ordinated, you will need much less. Everything will mix and match beautifully, and you won't need one of everything in every color.

Finally, to be your most beautiful, you must get organized. Organize your time, your home, and your closet. Yes, organize your life! It may take a while to get it all done, but begin. The Lord's ambassador should not represent sloppiness and chaos. God is a God of perfect order. If He could organize the universe, we should be able, with His help, to organize our little corner of the world.

The more we get our time and possessions under control, the more we can accomplish. And, most importantly, the more time we can spend with our family. The more time you have to spend with your husband, the more you will see him bloom. A man can't help but be pleased to be the object of attention of a beautiful woman like you.

That is why God sent you to be an ambassador of Christ to your husband.

# 4

# RESPECTING YOUR HUSBAND

*"Nevertheless let each individual among you also love his own wife even as himself; and let the wife see to it that she respect her husband"*— Ephesians 5:33.

Have you ever wondered why the Bible repeatedly tells men to love their wives but only tells wives to respect their husbands? Perhaps it is because men and women tend to understand "love" differently. Women seem to associate loving someone with doing things for them— laundry, cooking, cleaning, etc. But men often take that kind of love for granted. They don't seem to correlate the benefit of all that effort with being loved.

But show me a man who feels respected by his wife, and I'll show you a man who feels loved. Respect is probably a man's most deep-down basic need. If that isn't fulfilled, he has no foundation to build upon. Give him everything the world values except respect, and a man feels that he has nothing. But give a man who has nothing respect, and he can conquer the world.

## The Tragedy Of Disrespect

A man who receives no respect is unable to receive love—from people or God—because he feels too unworthy. Comedian Rodney Dangerfield gets laughs by moaning, "I don't get no respect." That line has touched something in his audience and made him famous. But his humor belies the real tragedy of men who never thrive because the most important woman in their lives won't show them respect.

A wife might actually feel respect for her husband; but unless she expresses it in a way that is meaningful to him, he won't know it is there. A man without respect feels worthless. He first loses his own self-esteem, then his ambition, and ultimately his desire to live. He may even have such self-hatred that he projects it onto others and strikes out in violence.

A good case in point is Lee Harvey Oswald. As a child he received little respect from his family. Always rejected by his peers as a schoolboy, he later received no respect from his own children. But the last straw was when he was repeatedly ridiculed and humiliated by his wife. Shooting the most respected man he knew—the president— was his desperate way of crying out for recognition.

If only one significant person in Oswald's life had shown him respect, perhaps President Kennedy would be alive today.

On the other hand, I know of a woman who persevered in showing respect to her husband through years of his alcoholism. He had suffered abuse as a child. When they married, his self-esteem was on the bottom, so he drank to ease the pain. Members of both his and her families urged her over and over to leave such an irresponsible, no-good man for her own sake, if not for the childrens'. They told her she was too good a person to be wasted on a selfish, drunken husband like that.

But this devoted wife let them all know that she would not tolerate such talk. Through many years of trials and tribulations she persisted in showing her husband how much she respected and believed in him, even though no one else thought he deserved it. Because his income was inconsistent, she had to work full time while rearing the children and keeping their home. She lovingly sewed his shirts on her sewing machine and never missed an opportunity to let him know how much she admired the good in him.

Today he is a recovered alcoholic and a real prize of a husband. He is living proof of the value that she saw in him all along. I am convinced that the respect this man received from his loving, faithful wife salvaged him from the scrap heap of society.

We are to respect our husband for his position as husband if not for his personality or position in life. We are not to respect him because he has done something to "deserve" it but because God's Word says to. We owe our president respect even if he isn't the candidate we voted for. We may not have loving feelings toward the police officer writing us a traffic ticket, but we had better show him respect for the position he holds. In the same way, we are to honor our husband without judging whether he is measuring up to our expectations. None of us can afford to be judged so harshly.

Respecting your husband is worth the effort. (1) You reap the rewards of being obedient to the Lord. (2) There are many fringe benefits in having a happy, contented husband. (3) It paves the way for your husband to believe God loves him because he trusts your love. (4) If you find all those "submits" in the Bible irksome, respecting your husband will make them quite palatable.

I used to cringe secretly every time I read "wives *submit* to your husbands" in God's Word. I thought, What a demeaning and oppressive thing to be told to do! But I have found that when I show respect to my husband, submission just tags along innocuously. When my husband says, "I'd like you to pick up a new license plate for my car this week" (not knowing that I already have twenty other things to do), I just say, "Okay." Then I put that job on the top of my priority list, not because I feel forced to "submit" but because I want to show my husband that I respect his wishes. Respect puts joy into submission, making it painless.

When your children see you showing respect to their father, it says more to them than a thousand sermons. Never tolerate a disrespectful word or attitude from them toward their father, even when he is wrong. Just say, "We always treat your father with respect, whether we agree with him or not, and I won't tolerate any other attitude." Your childrens' own self-esteem depends upon having a father they respect.

### Criticism Vs. Respect

One Christian woman I know has a bad habit of harshly correcting her husband in front of others. If she cared about showing him respect, she would wait for a quiet moment when they were alone to discuss the issue. I suspect that is one reason why their relationship is often strained and why she feels unfulfilled. An unhappy husband does not make for a fulfilling marriage.

Another snare to beware of is getting caught up in a gripe session with other women who are complaining about their husbands. It is easy to say something that you will later regret—"Why on earth did I say that? I didn't even mean it."

Negative talk is extremely contagious. Walking away when you first realize the drift of the conversation is much better.

Be especially careful not to discuss personal problems about your husband with other Christians for the sake of "praying about it." If you need a confidante to agree with you in prayer, find *one* trustworthy, mature Christian friend (of the same sex) with whom you can share special concerns. If your husband senses that his personal habits are written on the top of everyone's prayer list, he will be too embarrassed to sit in the same pew with them. Respect him by not violating his privacy.

Another way of showing respect to your husband is to compliment him on his good points. At one time I felt there was nothing admirable about which to compliment my husband. So I prayed, "Father, I'm sure I am just looking at the negative rather than the positive. Please bring to my heart an awareness and appreciation for the good things in my husband." Immediately, thoughts started coming: "He goes to work faithfully every day; he pays all the bills; he plays with the children; he is handsome; he loves you very much . . ." and on and on. I had plenty to compliment him on that night.

It does more than you can imagine to encourage your husband with a few kind words of love and appreciation. Knowing that he can expect to come home to a hug, a few tender words, and a good dinner makes his everyday drudgery worthwhile.

Once my husband and I were watching a movie in which a woman was instructing someone on how to care for her cat while she was gone. "Feed him and hug him everyday," she said. My husband smiled at me and said, "That sounds like good advice." Give a man those things, and he will feel like a king. It doesn't take much to make your man feel respected.

## An Attitude Of Heart

If you feel convicted by anything I have mentioned, join the club. This is the voice of experience speaking. It took me years to learn the importance of respecting my husband. Even after we wives have learned this spiritual principle, we all still fail at times. The important thing is being willing to obey God in this area.

Before my husband was saved, there were times I became disappointed in him and felt justified in not respecting him. I didn't feel able to respect him. But I learned that respect is not an emotion—it is an attitude of the heart. It is the way you act, not the way you feel. Just as our salvation does not depend upon our day-to-day feelings, neither does our ability to treat our husbands with respect. If you are obedient in *acting* respectful toward your husband, you can trust God to supply the respectful *feelings,* too.

My friend, Vinita, is from India, and her parents arranged her marriage when she was a young woman. I have always admired how beautifully she shows respect to her husband, whether he is home or away on a business trip. She constantly thinks of him, doing things she knows will please him. I have never been able to tempt her into anything that would interfere with her getting a good dinner on the table at the end of the day. But the most impressive thing is the deep love they show for one another.

One day I remarked how fortunate she was that her parents had arranged her marriage to a man that she obviously loved so much.

"Oh, I did not love him at first," she laughed. "I did not even know him. The love—that comes later!"

In her culture a woman is taught from infancy to show respect to her husband. How else could two married strangers fall in love?

Do you feel as if you and your husband are strangers? Are you distant from one another—living in two different worlds? Is it possible that you have become separated by your failed expectations and creeping criticisms? Respect must be restored in your marriage before anything else can grow. You, as a Christian wife, can be the one to restore mutual respect to your marriage.

Just as a garden needs to be both weeded and watered, respect can only grow where criticism has been uprooted and praise and respect are applied daily. Nobody ever said gardening was easy, but the fruit of your efforts will be worth it.

# 5

# HOW TO WITNESS WITHOUT A WORD

*"In the same way, you wives, be submissive to your own husbands so that even if any of them are disobedient to the word, they may be won without a word by the behavior of their wives, as they observe your chaste and respectful behavior"*—1 Peter 3:1-2.

I know a Christian man who got saved before his wife did, early in their marriage. He was joyous to know the Lord but at the same time miserable because of his wife. She thought his "religion" was foolish and embarrassing. The more he tried to convince her to ask Jesus into her heart, the more stubbornly she resisted. It soon became a tormenting test of wills, but he was determined to win.

"I came home from work every night and started telling her about the Lord and why she must become a Christian," he said. "I made her sit and listen to me as I read the Bible. I refused to give in. It was the longest and most miserable three months of my life, but she finally got saved."

Today he is a pastor, and she is a lovely, supportive pastor's wife. Their ministry together is beautiful. When he told me how he practically forced his wife to become a Christian and how it only took three "long" months, I thought maybe that is the way to get one's mate saved. After all, I had been waiting patiently for many years for my husband to get saved, and he hadn't budged.

But, after some prayer and meditation, I knew there was *no way* my husband would ever put up with being force-fed Christianity. Why? Because the Lord created a man to be the spiritual leader of his family. What may work on a woman won't necessarily work on a man. He just isn't made to be his wife's follower, even if she is right and he is wrong. The more a wife tries to tell the average, normal husband why he should get saved, the more he is going to resist. That is why the Bible wisely tells us to witness to our husbands "without a word." If you don't say it, he can't resist it. But if he sees you acting like a Christian, without preaching, that will speak volumes.

Does that mean you can't even talk about spiritual things if your husband initiates the conversation? Of course not. If he asks a question, give him a simple, direct answer. But resist the impulse to take advantage of the opportunity by jumping in with a theological dissertation ending with an invitation to ask Jesus into his heart. Just answer

40

the question. Don't manipulate your conversations toward a spiritual slant. People know when they are being manipulated, and they resent it.

## Walking The Walk

It is human nature to resist anything you feel is being forced upon you. If you think someone is trying too hard to be your friend, it is human nature to feel like holding back. If someone starts showering you with compliments, you will probably start suspecting their motives. When you were a schoolgirl, was there ever a boy who had a crush on you and followed you around like a puppy, begging for your attention? Wasn't he a turn-off? The more someone pushes something at you, the more you feel like pushing back or running the other way.

If your husband finds you overly eager to tell him about God, he is naturally going to feel like pulling away, not only from God but from you. Moping about with a sad face because of his rejection will only worsen things. Leaving little tracts around the house or an open Bible on his nightstand will probably drive him up the wall or out of the house.

Behavior that says, "Here's Jesus; please, *please* take Him!" only cheapens the gospel. If Jesus Christ is really as wonderful as we think He is, then He doesn't need to be peddled like a vacuum sweeper. Hard sell is not necessary. The problem

41

is that people want to tell about Jesus rather than *show* Jesus. Ever hear the expression, "He wants to talk the talk, but doesn't walk the walk"? To witness most effectively to our husbands we need to "walk the walk, not-talk the talk."

Another important reason to "witness without words" is that you don't want your husband to think he is resisting you when he is really resisting God. It is tempting to try and play the part of the Holy Spirit by trying to convict others with our arguments and backing them into a corner with pointed scriptures. But to a man who is not ready to receive the conviction of the Holy Spirit, that can be like waving a flag in front of a bull— he will only see red.

"Do not give what is holy to dogs, and do not throw your pearls before swine, lest they trample them under their feet, and turn and tear you to pieces," Jesus said in Matthew 7:6. If you are getting ahead of the Holy Spirit, be prepared to be trampled right along with the Word of God.

It isn't that your husband intends to be hostile about spiritual things—he just doesn't yet have the ability to understand them. As a result, he may feel threatened and react out of a secret sense of inadequacy. 1 Corinthians 2:12,14 says,

> Now we have received, not the spirit
> of the world, but the Spirit who is from
> God, that we might know the things
> freely given to us by God . . . But a

natural man does not accept the things of the Spirit of God; for they are foolishness to him, and he cannot understand them, because they are spiritually appraised.

## An Unprepared Vessel

Years ago, my neighbor, Diane, had to call the apartment maintenance man to repair her leaky kitchen faucet. While checking the defective faucet, he noticed that the drain pipe under the sink was leaking, too. So he removed the drain pipe and put a bucket under the sink to catch the drips while he went to the store for new parts.

Hours later Diane noticed that the maintenance man had not yet returned and went to check the bucket under the sink. To her alarm she found the bucket not only full of water, but on the verge of overflowing onto the floor. Thankful that she had found the bucket in time to prevent a mess, she very slowly lifted the bucket out from the cabinet and inched it up over the counter.

Finally, with a sigh of relief, Diane dumped the water into the sink. It wasn't until she noticed her wet feet that she realized what she had done!

We laughed ourselves silly over that story. It's always funny when we catch ourselves doing some automatic, mindless act with absurd consequences—like throwing dirty socks into the toilet instead of the clothes hamper.

But Christian wives need to be careful about automatically talking "spiritual talk" to their unsaved husbands. It's such a natural response, sometimes, to talk to your husband about the Lord like you would to a good Christian friend. But the consequences can be much the same as pouring water into a sink with no drain pipe. Your words run right through and make a mess because there isn't a proper vessel to receive them.

You can be left feeling quite foolish when your well-meant words have produced only a resentful, turned-off husband—kind of like Diane felt as she stood there in a puddle of her own making. It isn't until your husband's heart is prepared and softened by the Holy Spirit that he can comprehend and appreciate spiritual concepts.

Above all, don't let your husband draw you into arguments about the Bible. If he disagrees with Scripture, just smile and say, "God said it, not me." That puts the ball back into your husband's court, forcing him to decide whether he wants to agree or disagree with God. But if you are defending Scripture, your husband has the perfect excuse for disagreeing with you, thus robbing the Holy Spirit of the opportunity to convict him.

## Watching And Waiting

In his excellent book, *Love Must Be Tough,* James Dobson makes an important observation about the marriage relationship. He says that when a man starts to feel trapped in his marriage, he will test his freedom by pulling away. The normal reaction for the wife is to try and cling more tightly to him. But this can be a critical mistake: It only confirms his suspicion that he is being held against his will and causes him to pull away even more.

The wise wife, Dr. Dobson explains, recognizes her husband's need to feel that his marriage is still based on freedom; therefore, she gives him space. When he pulls away, she doesn't chase after him but rather acts calm and unconcerned. This reaction surprises her husband and causes him to feel he is allowed to make his own choices in the relationship and is not being crowded or coerced. Consequently, he feels safe in drawing close to his wife again.

Let's apply Dr. Dobson's observations to the situation of a Christian woman trying to win her husband to Christ. A woman must avoid the appearance of chasing her husband with the gospel at all cost. If she senses resistance to anything she has said pertaining to her faith, she should immediately pull back and be quiet about the subject altogether. It may take weeks, months, or longer before her husband feels unthreatened enough to open himself up to his wife spiritually. In the meantime, by manifesting a "gentle and quiet spirit" and letting Jesus be seen in her attitudes and actions, the wife is building a bridge of trust upon which she and her husband can meet at a later, more opportune time.

Remember, it was through "faith and patience" that our forefathers "inherited the promises" of God. (See Hebrews 6:12.) God is faithful to those who trust and wait. By refraining from speaking about your faith and concentrating on the verse, "I will show you my faith by my works" (James 2:18), you will take your husband off the defensive.

Your husband may be expecting to be badgered about going to church or reading the Bible. When you don't say a word, he will at first be greatly relieved. Then, as he sees you growing in peace and joy, he may become curious. But don't speak up yet. The cardinal rule of bargaining is, "The first one to make an offer loses." It's a waiting game. Let him stew until he can stand the quiet no more and comes to you with his questions or offers to go to church.

Like drawing a bee with honey, sweetness is more persuasive than picking and probing. Watch and wait. Peace is better than war, and a calm home atmosphere is better than one of conflict. You can witness in either one, but why not do it the easy way?

The best reason for witnessing without words is that when the day does come when it is right for you to say something about the Lord to your husband, your words will carry much more impact. Have you ever "tuned out" someone who talks too much? Even if they said something profound you would never notice it amidst all their wordiness. But when a quiet person speaks, people listen. Each word becomes a gem. Try letting your words be solitary gems. Meanwhile, enjoy being one yourself, and let your witness sparkle in silence.

# 6

# HIS POINT OF VIEW

*"Do not be bound together with unbelievers; for what partnership have righteousness and lawlessness, or what fellowship has light with darkness? Or what harmony has Christ with Belial, or what has a believer in common with an unbeliever?"*—2 Corinthians 6:14-15.

Is it hard for you to understand what goes on in your husband's brain whenever he acts sullen and withdrawn because he resents your "religion"? What could prompt the same man who said, "I do," and carried you away to live happily ever-after to do his best, now, to make your life unbearable? How could he be so unkind? Doesn't he love you anymore?

I found those questions difficult to answer, too. That's why I had to ask my husband about it after he became a born-again Christian. "What made you act so difficult?" I asked. "Why did you resent my faith so terribly?"

His answers showed me that the spiritual incompatability spoken of in 2 Corinthians 6:14-15 was just as painful for him as it was for me. In fact, perhaps it was even more difficult for him because, while we lived in separate worlds, it was he who lived in darkness.

Mark's expression saddened as he recaptured memories of the feelings he had experienced when we were separated by the same Holy Spirit who now makes us so close. He spoke with great emotion as he tried to explain the point of view of an unsaved man whose wife is a Christian.

"You have to remember what it's like when a man marries his wife," he said. "She is more than his lover—she's his whole life and his first priority. He never wants anything to come between the two of them.

"A man can have trouble accepting his own children because each new child takes so much of his wife's affection away from him. Suddenly, her main concern is for the children rather than for him. The only way he can tolerate their intrusion into his marriage relationship is that *he* also comes to know and love them.

"But when a man's wife becomes a Christian, it's a whole different kind of threat. Suddenly she has a love relationship with someone he can't even see. He can't understand anything she tries to tell him about this new God she has come to know.

"All he knows is that she's in love with somebody else, and he is jealous. Instead of remaining the first priority in her life as when they first got married, he has suddenly been demoted to number two after God. That is the way it must be for a Christian, but an unbelieving husband can't understand that at all. It would be easier for him to understand if she had run off with another man; but she's in love with someone he can't even compete with. He feels helpless.

"To make matters worse, she starts pressuring him to love her God, too. That really makes him resentful. It's worse than if, after he had gotten married, his mother-in-law moved in, and she and his wife took sides against him.

"When she finds that she is unable to share her greatest joy with her husband, the wife starts craving 'fellowship.' She can't wait to be with her Christian friends every chance she gets. And she suddenly loses interest in her old friends because they aren't Christians. So now the man and wife don't even have friends in common anymore.

"The husband feels that he hasn't changed— *she* has. She has broken the marriage contract. In his eyes, she is being unfaithful.

"The sad thing," Mark said, "is that the more he loves his wife, the harder he fights the one thing that could bring them closer together—her faith."

### A Delicate Balance

Reflecting on all the times that I felt Mark's rejection was a sign of how much he disapproved of me, I realized it was just his feeling of betrayal that caused him to withdraw emotionally. I asked Mark what a wife should do to help avoid those feelings in her husband.

"Most of all she needs to be sure her need for Christian fellowship doesn't circumvent her relationship with her husband. She should try to fit all that in when he's at work or some other time when the husband and wife ordinarily wouldn't be together.

"She should try to keep her priorities (1) God, (2) husband, (3) children, (4) church and fellowship—in that order. When she feels rejected by her husband, she has a tendency to switch priority number two with number four. That's definitely a mistake. Rather than being with her husband less, she should double the time she spends with him so he can't complain about being abandoned.

"And the time she spends with him should not be used to try talking him into becoming a Christian. She should just let her husband see Jesus in her while she spends more time with him."

Admittedly that is a tall order to fill for a woman whose husband is pushing her away out of fear of being more hurt. He secretly desires more time and a closer relationship with her, yet he sends her signals that say, "Keep out of my life."

Once I confided in a letter to a friend how very rejected I felt by my husband. Needing to release the hurt somehow, and feeling safe in telling it to a friend far away, I thought she would return some advice or consolation.

Instead, by return mail, I received a stern rebuke for saying negative things about my husband, followed by this advice, "Just do everything together like my husband and I do."

It hurt to realize that my friend, who enjoyed a great relationship with her Christian husband, was incapable of comprehending being married to a husband who won't allow you into his life—a relationship so devoid of companionship that it seemed like living death.

I started to write back and try to explain, but, after a few attempts, I crumpled the paper. I couldn't bear to admit, "I can't share any part of my husband's life. And he doesn't want any part of mine. We literally live in two different worlds, and it hurts more than I can say.

"He doesn't want to be near me. He won't even let me ride in the car with him to the corner store. And when we're together at home, I'm lonelier than when he is away because his presence reminds me how distant we have become.

"We can't even talk to each other. Our words fall to the ground like dead leaves and just lie there. Everything is empty and hollow. I ache to hold him in my arms and feel close, but even that doesn't penetrate our separateness. I wish to God that we could, 'do everything together.'"

So there we were, both Mark and I wanting more than anything in the world to be close to each other but separated by a wall of hurt and misunderstanding. Even though our relationship did improve over the years, that wall was always vaguely there.

That wall never entirely disappeared until after Mark became a Christian, too. Then we became just as close as we had always wished we could be—as close as I had always sensed was possible if he knew the Lord.

## Unconditional Love

Many people try to make unequally yoked wives feel better by telling them that marriage between an unequally yoked couple is "really not all that different" from a Christian marriage. This is an unfair exaggeration to make. *Of course* it is different, or the Bible would not warn Christians against entering into such a union.

Such advice can make a Christian wife feel guilty for feeling that she wants more out of her relationship with her husband. She may sense that she and her husband aren't quite as soul-to-soul close as some Christian couples she has observed. And she may be right in sensing that. Most Christians will admit that they feel closer to their Christian friends than they do to their non-Christian friends. If that is true in a friendship, how much truer might it be in a marriage?

But an unequally yoked marriage can be a very good marriage, just as a friendship with an unbeliever can be a very good friendship. Once you get past the honeymoon, friendship is the basis for a good marriage. So that, in essence, is what an unequally yoked wife needs to strive for in her marriage—a deeper friendship with her husband.

Hopefully this chapter will help you understand where your husband is coming from so your friendship can thrive a little better. My mother says, "I love ya—warts and all!" That's what real friendship is all about, isn't it?

In the meantime you can be sure that God is working behind the scenes to bring your husband to know Him at the earliest possible opportunity. If, like most husbands, your husband cannot receive spiritual direction from you, his wife, don't worry. God will find someone to plant the gospel in his heart when he least expects it.

I know of one man whose wife prayed for him for years with no results. Then one day while he was on a business trip he was brought to Christ by a fellow traveler in an airport. This man actually stood there in the terminal and, crying unashamedly, prayed for Jesus to come into his heart. By the time he got home, he was so euphoric over meeting the Lord that his wife accused him of being drunk! Today he is a powerful soul winner.

Sometimes a man's pride just won't allow him to receive spiritual truth from those he is closest to. Once I asked Mark why my example never caused him to accept the Lord.

"It couldn't," he answered, "because I resented your faith too much. I never understood that your faith is what made you such a good wife and mother. I just expected you to be that way. Only after I became a Christian did I realize the truth. And now I appreciate it. Most of all, I appreciate you for raising our children to be Christians when I didn't care. I can never thank you enough for that."

It was our sons, after all, who brought their father to the Lord. As a registered nurse, I was at work one Sunday, when Scot, then sixteen, and Todd, thirteen, talked their father into going to church with them. Mark responded to the altar call, and the boys resolutely stood beside him and accompanied him to the front of the church to pray for salvation. You never know whom God will use to bring your husband to the Lord!

Until that time, take heart in knowing that your husband does love you even when he seems unlovable. Don't entertain thoughts of giving up—this is just the beginning of a great future! Take courage, build on what you have, and try to understand things from his point of view.

# 7

# OVERCOMING PERSECUTION

*"If they persecuted Me, they will also persecute you"*—John 15:20.

The wife of an unbeliever is dependent upon God's grace to get her through each day; she is under pressure from every direction. On one hand she is under duress by her husband, who may think she has a mental problem—one of those "religious fanatics." On the other hand the church may be sending her subtle but stressful messages that she must not be doing things right; otherwise her husband would be a believer by now.

Then she has the inevitable flack from friends, family members, or co-workers who think she has become some kind of cult member for having a faith that affects her way of life. If, in addition to that, her own children are against her "religion," she is truly an alien in her own home.

All the persecution in the world would be much more easily borne if only she had the support of an understanding mate on her side. But bearing it alone only magnifies the difficulty. On top of that, her own husband's disapproval becomes the heaviest load of all, at times crushing her spirit and snuffing her joy.

But rejoice! The hotter the fire, the stronger the temper of the steel! It is these very pressures that turn wives of unbelievers into indomitable towers of faith. Face it—that kind of pressure is guaranteed either to make you or break you. Nobody is going to maintain her Christian stance under all that intense heat unless she really has a grip on God.

Persecution weeds out half-committed Christians like bug spray cleans up a picnic—wishy-washy believers drop like flies. Anyone who has been a Christian for any length of time has seen new converts come and go, from popular rock stars to the gal in Bible study who got saved but then dropped out because her friends thought it was "too weird."

Such people make a big splash about conversion when they desperately need God and He meets their needs. But once their problems are solved, or they get a taste of being ostracized by the world for being "different," these half-hearted believers back off in a hurry. They want to be secret Christians so the world will still accept them. These fair weather friends of God—clouds without rain—seeds sown on rocky soil—are a sad, but true, fact of life.

# The Apple Of God's Eye

Women who remain faithful to Christ and an unbelieving husband at the same time are a higher caliber of Christian. As different as gold is from plastic, they are the kind of women that give God great joy—the apple of His eye. They are God's delight, and He loves them in the same special way that He loved Daniel for walking into the lions' den or Shadrach, Meshach, and Abed-nego for submitting themselves to the fiery furnace rather than denying their Lord.

Just as God was there in the midst of trial for Daniel and his friends, He is there for you. You can never be more faithful to the Father than He will be to you in return. Never. Only He knows the particular suffering you endure in your marriage on His account, and only He can reward you for it. But reward you He will:

> "Blessed are those who have been persecuted for the sake of righteousness, for theirs is the kingdom of heaven. Blessed are you when men cast insults at you, and persecute you, and say all kinds of evil against you falsely, on account of Me. Rejoice, and be glad, for your reward in heaven is great, for so they persecuted the prophets who were before you"—Matthew 5:10-12.

The rewards of being faithful to Christ through persecution are worth more than all the approval and adulation the world can offer. (If the world's approval was so great, how many of us would have gone seeking after God in the first place?) Neither the world nor even our dear husbands can offer the security and peace that is freely ours in Christ.

It is difficult for me to recall just how desolate the "old" me was before I gave my life to Christ. I can only vaguely recall the despair, emptiness, and purposelessness of my former life. But I remember it enough to know that, by His grace, I'll cling to God with every ounce of strength in me, face any danger or ridicule, or lose everything the world has to offer rather than go back to that darkness.

## Divine Endurance

Those who have never tasted persecution can never know the rewards granted in its midst. The wife of an unsaved husband develops a resilience and tenacity in her faith that she never would have dreamed possible. God gives strength as it is needed.

> But we have this treasure in earthen
> vessels, that the surpassing greatness of
> the power may be of God and not from
> ourselves; we are afflicted in every way,
> but not crushed; perplexed, but not

despairing; persecuted, but not forsaken; struck down, but not destroyed—2 Corinthians 4:7-9.

The more you call upon God out of weakness and need, the more He gives you unshakable faith and endurance. While reading the incredible testimonies of Christians in Russia who, although tortured and imprisoned, stood firm in their faith, I wondered, Would I measure up in such a situation? Could I ever be that strong and faithful to God? I secretly feared that if I were in their place I would buckle at the first threat of physical or mental discomfort.

But now I have confidence that I would not. Sounds conceited, right? Quite the contrary. After years of marriage to an unbeliever, I know beyond the shadow of a doubt that God never expects anything of us that He does not first equip us for. I know it was God who gave me the strength to stand when the going got tough. It was His grace that allowed me to rise up where I would, of myself, have surely fallen. I have no illusions about myself. Without the grace of God, I could never have run the race, let alone finish as a winner, on that difficult course.

Now that my husband is a believer, I know I deserve no credit for his conversion. God kept me in the faith, and God brought my husband into the faith. The victory always goes to Christ, the perfector and finisher of our faith! (See Hebrews 12:2.)

Even though being the Christian wife of an unbeliever does not compare to physical torture behind the Iron Curtain, it can be emotional torture and should not be taken lightly. The more sensitive the wife, or the more insensitive the husband, the tougher life can be. It was murder for a cream puff like me.

Persecution drove me desperately close to God, and for that I am thankful. If my first years of being a born-again Christian had been all fun and laughter, I may very well have floated away from God on my little cloud of euphoria. There's nothing like having real hurts and needs, and seeing God take care of each one, to strengthen your faith and gratitude to Him. Nothing compares with watching God be strong in you, when you know you're a jellyfish inside.

The first century Christians were thrown to the lions and forced to worship in catacombs, but they also healed the sick, raised the dead, and carried the gospel to the world. No pain, no gain. The obstacles they had to overcome made them giants of faith.

Is your horizon full of mountains? Are you aching and lonely for a spiritual relationship with your husband? Are you often misunderstood or rejected for your faith? Do you, time and again, fail at being the "perfect" wife and Christian? Then again, I say, rejoice! Those are just the stepping-stones to glory.

"For momentary, light affliction is producing for us an eternal weight of glory far beyond all comparison" (2 Corinthians 4:17).

*You're becoming an overcomer!*

# 8

# TAMING TEMPTATION

*"Beloved, do not be surprised at the fiery ordeal among you, which comes upon you for your testing, as though some strange thing were happening to you"*—1 Peter 4:12.

One fiery ordeal common to Christian women with unsaved husbands—but almost never discussed—is the temptation to marital infidelity. This should come as no shock or cause undue alarm. Neither should the fact be locked up behind great walls of silence and denial. The devil works in darkness. Let's expose his deeds to the light and thus disarm him of one of his cruelest weapons.

## Loneliness And Despair

Satan uses many fiery darts to tempt women into infidelity, but loneliness is probably chief among them. The wife of an unbeliever has a spiritual hunger for a Christian mate that can cause her to ache with loneliness even when her husband is sitting right next to her. Proverbs 13:12 says, "Hope deferred makes the heart sick," and that's what she is—heartsick.

Jesus said, "For this cause a man shall leave his father and mother, and shall cleave to his wife; and the two shall become one flesh. Consequently they are no longer two, but one flesh" (Matthew 19:5-6).

This is the way it is and should be. But when a woman receives the indwelling presence of the Holy Spirit and her mate does not, it can cause painful disunity and searing disharmony. Once they were both spiritually dead but equally united in the flesh. Now she is spiritually alive and suddenly needing—craving—to be united with her husband in that dimension as well.

I once wrote in my diary, "I must be one flesh with a husband who is spiritually dead. I must be mother and spiritual authority to our two young sons while having no spiritual authority of my own. I must be a strong woman who stands firmly on her convictions in spite of being pulled at and torn from every side—I must do it all alone."

Such a climate can create an emotional bind for a woman—for a good reason. God's ideal plan is that a man and a woman be one in body, soul, and spirit, just as He is one in the Father, Son, and Holy Spirit. Love must share itself; that is a God-given desire. A wife wants more than anything to share God's love with her husband. But the more she tries to share it, the more he resists. He is resisting the gospel, but she feels that he is rejecting her.

This situation sets the stage for temptation to enter her life. Satan, that predictable old fox, steps in and says, "That woman is walking around with a bleeding heart, desperate to find a soul mate. I'll supply her with one myself!"

If she is unaware of the enemy's deceptions, the wife of an unbeliever is wide open for the first opportunist who happens along. He usually takes the form of a spiritual man or authority figure upon whom she can project her dreams of the ideal man. He may be a minister, a counselor, her doctor, or anyone she encounters who seems genuinely concerned for her. She may feel that this man finds her attractive, appreciates her inner beauty, and shares her spiritual desires. A little demonic "Cupid" pierces her heart with a fiery dart.

### Enduring Temptation

If things get to this point before the woman realizes she is experiencing spiritual warfare with the devil, her battle will be uphill. It is much easier to fight temptation before becoming deeply emotionally involved. But once a Christian woman wakes up and puts on the spiritual armor of Ephesians 6, she can always be victorious over temptation. Satan is already a defeated foe, vanquished two thousand years ago by the shed blood of Jesus Christ. We have only to realize this truth and apply it to our own situation.

At this point a woman needs to remind herself of two important truths. (1) It is not a sin to be tempted. Jesus was tempted, too. ''For we do not have a high priest who cannot sympathize with our weaknesses but one who has been tempted *in all things as we are,* yet without sin'' (Hebrews 4:15, *Italics added*). But once you realize that you are being tempted, willfull indulgence in thoughts or actions provoked by that temptation is sin. (2) Resisting sin is not necessarily going to be easy, but that is no excuse for going ahead with sinning. You *can* overcome every temptation; God's Word says so:

> No temptation has overtaken you but such as is common to man; and God is faithful, who will not allow you to be tempted beyond that you are able, but with the temptation will provide the way of escape also, that you may be able to endure it—1 Corinthians 10:13.

Notice that you must ''endure it.'' Does that sound easy? I always thought fighting temptation should be easy for a Christian, and finding out that it was often difficult shocked me. I thought something was wrong with me until I read these scriptures. Denying the flesh is not necessarily easy.

Giving up your hopes and dreams of being rescued by your white knight can be difficult, but it is easier than living with the consequences of sin.

Only someone who has never endured real temptation can act smug about those who have. I was very humbled to learn how weak the flesh is through such experiences. But I also learned that through my weakness God can be strong. And the greater the temptation, the more glory He receives when we triumph over it through the power of Jesus Christ.

> Be sober of spirit, be on the alert. Your adversary, the devil, prowls about like a roaring lion, seeking someone to devour. But resist him, firm in your faith, knowing that the same experiences of suffering are being accomplished by your brethren who are in the world. And after you have suffered for a little while, the God of all grace, who called you to His eternal glory in Christ, will Himself perfect, confirm, strengthen and establish you—1 Peter 5:8-10.

Yes, resisting temptation can cause "suffering," but not nearly the suffering that would result from giving in to it. A family torn apart by infidelity is a tragedy. It grieves God to see a woman shipwreck her husband, her children, and herself for the self-gratification of adultery. Proverbs 14:1 says, "The wise woman builds her house, but the foolish tears it down with her own hands."

If you have already fallen into the sin of adultery, what should you do? First, know that *God loves you* and died on the cross so that you could be forgiven. Accept His forgiveness, and then forgive yourself. Secondly, *repent,* which means, "Go and sin no more," as Jesus said to the woman caught in adultery. (See John 8.) He did not accuse her. He just forgave her and set her free to live as if she had never sinned. She started a whole new life. Some people think she was Mary Magdalene, the first person that Jesus appeared to after He rose from the dead. Be like this woman and turn away from sin and toward Jesus.

## Emotional Nakedness

It's one thing to avoid temptation, but suffering in silence all alone is not the answer, either. Women get involved with other men when they are lonely. If they don't get involved with other men, that doesn't make life any less lonely. There must be another alternative.

First, devote your energy to finding new ways to develop more closeness and communication with your husband. Nurture your friendship with him, and find common activities to share and enjoy together. Don't lose hope and give up.

It takes years for a marriage to develop to its fullest potential. Many Christian books can help you in this area—and Christian counselors as well.

Secondly, you must realize that there are no perfect marriages and no perfect husbands. When your husband becomes a Christian, he will not be perfect. There will still be areas to work on in your relationship. My husband was basically the same after he got saved, even though many wonderful changes had occurred in him. I was surprised to learn that my friends' Christian husbands, whom I had always admired and wanted *my* husband to be like, were not all perfect, either. It is an illusion that the grass is greener on the other side of the fence. You are just too far away to see the weeds.

Thirdly, you must learn to *let Jesus fulfill every need* that you can't satisfy at this time in your own marriage relationship. I am convinced that what every woman craves in her marriage is not better sex or romance but intimacy—total intimacy. Let me explain.

When I was six years old I fell in love with my first movie star, Alan Ladd. When I saw how handsome he was and how lovingly he treated his leading lady, it was all over—my first heartthrob. Our "affair" lasted for years.

Then I met Paul Newman. Oh, the ecstasy, the excitement those blue eyes provoked. My crush on Paul was serious, until I saw—who else?— Robert Redford! Every succeeding Redford movie made me weaker with desire. By this time I had gotten married, and I loved my husband very much. But occasionally I wondered, What if I had to choose between my husband and Robert Redford? Laugh all you want; but this was heavy infatuation and sexual attraction!

Now I am in my late thirties and, I'll admit, still a little in awe of Robert Redford. But I have learned the secret that makes each of those movie stars so attractive. It isn't his looks, his body, or even his personality. It is the way he looks right into your eyes from up there on that big screen and becomes totally intimate—soul to soul—with you. He is vulnerable. He is open and candid. There is nothing held back, nothing between you. You can read every emotion he is experiencing. The best way I can describe this is to call it *emotional nakedness*. This, I believe, is what a woman desires in her relationship with her husband.

Unfortunately, in our society men are trained to be just the opposite. They must be strong and brave and know it all. They must be anything but vulnerable, especially to the woman who depends on them. They can't admit, even to themselves, their need for intimacy with a wife or with God.

Have you ever seen a man walking down the aisle at an altar call with tears streaming down his face, oblivious to whoever may be watching? That person is experiencing emotional nakedness with God. Perhaps for the first time he has let down the barriers and said, ''Look at me just as I am, with nothing to hide behind. No more games. God, I need You." Now begins a real relationship with God.

## Completion In Christ

If your relationship with your husband is not yet close enough and trusting enough to have the emotional nakedness it takes to become truly intimate, keep working at it. Don't seek it in another man, romance novels, or soap operas. Those are cheap, unsatisfying imitations. In the meantime, you can have that one-to-one intimacy, just like lovers do, with the One who loves you most of all—Jesus Christ.

Do you want to look into someone's eyes and have them look back into yours? Then look into Jesus' eyes. Do you want to hold someone and be held? Hold onto Jesus. Do you want to tell someone about your dreams and hopes and fears? Tell Jesus. Then sit quietly and learn to hear the words He whispers to your heart.

> "Fear not, for you will not be put to shame; neither feel humiliated, for you will not be disgraced; but you will forget the shame of your youth, and the reproach of your widowhood you will remember no more.
> "For your husband is your Maker, Whose name is the Lord of hosts; and

your Redeemer is the Holy One of Israel, Who is called the God of all the earth.

"For the Lord has called you, like a wife forsaken and grieved in spirit, even like a wife of one's own youth when she is rejected," says your God—Isaiah 54:4-6.

Yes, you may be a spiritual widow right now, but until your husband becomes alive in Christ, your spiritual husband is Jesus. When you are lonely, run into His arms. You will find a special tenderness in your union with Him too personal and tangible for words to explain. God's compensation to you for your spiritual widowhood is a beautiful, intimate relationship with Christ. He is your All-in-All. He is your Lover.

# 9

# THE KEYS OF THE KINGDOM

*"The effectual fervent prayer of a righteous man availeth much"*—James 5:16 *KJV*.

Do you feel that your prayers for your husband's salvation are "availing much"? If not, it may be that your prayers are either not "effectual" or not "fervent." Mine were tearful, heart-wrenching prayers flung desperately toward heaven when I felt I could no longer bear the spiritual chasm between my husband and myself. My prayers were fervent, to say the least, but they didn't seem to avail much until I also learned the secret of praying effectually.

If you pray like I did, you may be praying, "Oh, Father in heaven, save my husband. Please, please, *please* save him!" Prayers of desperation, I call them—pleading, begging prayers—prayers that assume we must twist God's arm to get Him to do what the Bible says He most wants to do: bring men to salvation.

On one hand, we do need to make our requests known to the Father in prayer. Just as the Old Testament priests could only offer up to God what had been given them by the people, Jesus can only intercede on our behalf with the prayers that we have sent to the Father in His name. So we need to intercede on our husbands' behalf with confidence that our prayers are being heard.

But those old desperation prayers are a bit of a contradiction, aren't they? Why should we repeatedly need to beg God to save our husbands? Has God changed His mind about not wanting any to perish, but for all to come to repentance, as stated in 2 Peter 3:9? No. God never changes:

> Every good thing bestowed and every perfect gift is from above, coming down from the Father of lights, with whom there is no variation, or shifting shadow—James 1:17.

Is it possible, then, that God does not hear us when we pray for our husbands' salvation? No. First John 5:14 says, "And this is the confidence which we have before Him, that, if we ask anything according to His will, He hears us."

The Bible states clearly that God's will is to save our husbands and that He never changes His will. It also says that He hears us when we pray for our husbands' salvation. Consequently, if we feel that our prayers are ineffective, perhaps we can do something to make our prayers effectual. We need to learn the secret of praying with *all* the power and authority that God has given us.

I think that when we pray, "Oh, God, save my husband. Release him from the deception of the devil. Open his eyes and his heart. Lord, get him saved!" God is in heaven saying, "I'm doing My part. Why don't you do yours? I gave you the keys to the Kingdom of heaven—use them!"

In Matthew 16:13-20 Jesus revealed Himself, through Peter, as "the Christ, the Son of the Living God." Upon this declaration of faith Jesus gave Peter and the other disciples—and every believer today—the keys to the Kingdom power and authority that Christ, Himself, had.

> "I will give you the keys of the king-
> dom of heaven; and whatever you shall
> bind on earth shall be bound in heaven,
> and whatever you shall loose on earth
> shall be loosed in heaven"—Matthew
> 16:19.

If you, as a blood-bought believer, apply that verse to your prayers, nothing will render them ineffectual. Jesus prayed, "Thy kingdom come, Thy will be done on earth as it is in heaven." (See Matthew 6:10.) God's Kingdom came when Jesus won authority over Satan on the cross. Is God's will being done in your life? If not, it may be because you are unaware of your right to use those mighty keys.

## The Name Of Jesus

Before Christ died on the cross, mankind was helpless against Satan's authority. Originally all authority and dominion over the earth were given to Adam by God in the Garden of Eden. But when Adam fell into sin, he forfeited all that authority over to Satan, who became, ''the prince of the power of the air'' (Ephesians 2:2). Thus sin, sickness, poverty, and, worst of all, unbelief and rebellion against God entered into the human race from that generation on.

But then came Jesus, who, by shedding His atoning blood on the cross, defeated Satan once and for all. Jesus took our sin on Himself so that we could take on His righteousness. Then He took back the spiritual authority and power that Satan had usurped and handed it back to all those who had accepted His atoning salvation.

That is the difference between us (Christians) and the unbelieving world. They are still helpless against the devil, but we are free from the power of sin. 1 John 5:19 says, ''We know that we are of God, and the whole world lies in the power of the evil one.'' But we, as Christians, have power *over* the evil one because ''greater is He who is in you than he who is in the world'' (1 John 4:4).

The only requirements for using the mighty keys of binding and loosing are that you are a born-again Christian and that you use them in the name of Jesus Christ. Always remember that it is the authority of Christ you are exercising and not your own. Just as a busy executive might give his secretary the authority to sign his name or speak in his place, we have been given authority to use the name of Jesus Christ. When the secretary acts with that authority, it is just as effective as if the executive had done it himself. So it is when we act in Jesus' name.

Is your husband bound in sin and unbelief today? You can use the authority that you have in Christ to pray for him. The results may be immediate, or you may have to persevere for a while. But if you use the keys of the Kingdom as Jesus wants you to, you *must* win against those spiritual forces of deception and interference intent on keeping him in unbelief.

Two things can keep your husband out of God's Kingdom: (1) deception or controlling spirits from the enemy, and (2) his own free will.

The Holy Spirit cannot freely impart the truth of Christ and His salvation to your husband until those hindering evil forces are bound. Only then is your husband free to make an informed choice for or against Christ.

While God will never help you manipulate your husband into His Kingdom, He greatly desires that you use the keys of the Kingdom to set your husband free to make a decision based on his own understanding rather than on the deception or control of Satan.

You, as his wife, may be the only person in the world with the compassion, understanding, and power to protect your spiritually helpless husband from forces that he does not even believe exist. That is why he needs you to do spiritual warfare for him, until he, too, is a Christian with "armor" of his own.

## Binding And Loosing

To pray using the keys of the Kingdom, you must remember two important words: "bind" and "loose." You must first *bind* the power of the enemy and then *loose* the power of the Holy Spirit. In Matthew 12:22-29, the Pharisees accused Jesus of casting out demons by the power of the devil. Jesus replied to them,

> "Any kingdom divided against itself is laid waste; and any city or house divided against itself shall not stand. And if Satan casts out Satan, he is divided against himself; how then shall his kingdom stand? And if I by Beelzebul cast out demons, by whom do your sons cast them out? Consequently they shall be your judges. But if I cast out demons by the Spirit of God, then the kingdom

of God has come upon you. Or how can anyone enter the strong man's house and carry off his property, unless he first binds the strong man? And then he will plunder his house."

It is important to realize that the enemy plunders our house by first "binding" us so we can't fight back. Your husband may be bound by a spirit of unbelief, pride, or rebellion against the truth or by some besetting sin. He might be also bound by negative attitudes in *you,* his wife. Your own anxiety, fear, or anger may be hindering the Holy Spirit from working in your husband's heart. Before praying for your husband, examine your own heart, confess any negative attitudes to God, and be rid of them. Then you can proceed to bind the devil from working in your husband's life.

The exact words you use don't really matter. There is no magic incantation. What does matter is that you realize the real authority you are using when you speak in Jesus' name. You may want to pray this way daily until you have a sense of spiritual release, feeling sure that every evil stronghold has been broken. Ephesians 6:12 says,

For our struggle is not against flesh and blood, but against the rulers, against the powers, against the world forces of this darkness, against the spiritual forces of wickedness in the heavenly places.

Here is an example of how to pray using the keys of the Kingdom. In the parentheses, you may want to change the words to suit your situation.

*"In the name of Jesus Christ and by the power of His shed blood, I now take authority over the power of Satan and every evil spirit that he has sent against my husband. By the power of the blood of Christ I bind every spirit of (unbelief, pride, rebellion against the truth) in my husband and cast them out. I forbid them ever to return, in the name of Jesus Christ. And in His name I now loose the power of the Holy Spirit to work in my husband's heart to bring conviction of sin, repentance unto salvation, and total submission to the Lordship of Jesus Christ.*

*"Father in heaven, I have released my husband from the power of the enemy and now present him to You and Your Kingdom, in the wonderful name of Your precious Son, Jesus Christ. To Him be the glory and honor forever, amen."*

This prayer can be modified to use for any person or situation. Ask God to increase your understanding of ways to use the keys of the Kingdom to do His will on earth. Then watch the walls of opposition crumble at the mighty name of Jesus Christ!

In my Bible, next to Matthew 18:18—"Truly I say to you, whatever you shall bind on earth shall be bound in heaven; and whatever you loose on earth shall be loosed in heaven''—are the words I wrote in the margin: ''Mark is loosed! 5-30-80.''

On December 19, 1982, my husband, Mark, answered the altar call at church and received new birth in Christ.

Satan fought long and hard to keep that precious soul in darkness, but he could not win. Jesus always wins!

# 10

# THE SECRET WEAPON

*"For our struggle is not against flesh and blood, but against the rulers, against the powers, against the world forces of this darkness, against the spiritual forces of wickedness in the heavenly places"*—Ephesians 6:12.

Years ago I went to my pastor with a deep, dark question. "How can a person tell if they are demon possessed?" I asked as casually as possible. The pastor tried to stifle a grin and asked perceptively, "Now what makes you think you are demon possessed?"

"It's my dreams," I blurted, earnestly. "Almost every night I'm awakened by a terrifying dream. In it, I meet a man who I think is an old friend, and we start talking. But then I notice his eyes; they are full of fiery rage, piercing me with their glare. His eyes start coming closer and closer to me—threateningly close. Then I realize they aren't just this man's eyes—they are demons glowering at me through his eyes, wanting to attack me. I get so frightened that I start shouting, 'I rebuke you in the name of Jesus!' as I back away. But they keep coming closer. So I shout louder and louder until my own voice wakes me up. Then I lie there frightened, wondering what could make me keep having that same dream.''

My pastor's smile had faded. ''Don't worry,'' he said. ''It isn't you that the demonic influence is coming from. It's who you are sleeping with.''

He was right, but I took small comfort in that. At the time, evil forces intent on keeping my husband in sin and unbelief were oppressing him heavily. His hostility against me and other Christians was frightening. And his depression was almost tangible, hanging about him like a dark cloud.

Once I confided to a friend, ''I'm afraid he's going to snap and do something awful. Sometimes I'm scared to be around him.'' He had never been the type to harm anyone, but I sensed and feared that he was on the brink of desperation. Demonic powers were rampantly at work trying to destroy my husband and, perhaps, anyone near him. It was the bleakest time of my life.

Through much prayer from Christian friends, the crisis of those haunting months slowly passed. Gradually, the darkness was overcome by the Light. I only wish I had known then what I know now about fighting demonic oppression. I call it my ''secret weapon.''

# The Blood Of Christ

I learned a unique, effective way to fight the powers of darkness while working as a labor and delivery nurse. One of my co-workers who was openly hostile toward me often slandered me behind my back. Unable to understand why she disliked me or what I should do about it, I began to dread each work day.

One day I arrived at work only to receive a torrent of verbal abuse from her that left me distraught. Finally managing to tear my self-esteem to shreds, she left me dissolved in tears. I cried out to God, "Why is she doing this to me?" After drying my eyes and blowing my nose, I asked the Lord, "Is it possible that nothing she is saying truly reveals the issue? Could this be a spiritual battle?"

Then I remembered the day she had asked me why I was a Christian. "Because we are all sinners in need of a Savior," I answered. "That is why Jesus had to die on the cross." It was after that conversation that her hostility had begun.

My thoughts were interrupted when I had to admit a new patient—a young woman in early labor with her first baby. Her contractions were slow, so I talked with her through her first stages of labor to help pass the time. I learned that she was a beautician and also a Christian. We talked happily about the Lord between her contractions.

Suddenly, out of the blue, she told me the following story. "I work at the beauty shop with a lot of unbelievers. Sometimes one of those gals starts giving me a hard time about one thing or another, and it doesn't make sense. But the Lord showed me what the problem was with people like that. It's not what the person is *saying* that's really the problem. No, *it's just that the devil in them hates the Holy Spirit in me.*

"The person giving me the hard time doesn't even know the real reason they are being hateful. They think they just don't like me. They can't even help it—they are a victim of the devil, being used for his purpose to persecute believers."

When she said that I got goosebumps. I had not told her that I was having the same problem and, in fact, had just finished asking God to help me understand why. God is so wonderful to answer our prayers immediately when we are desperate for an answer. I thanked Him for sending my answer through the wisdom of this young woman.

She continued, "Whenever that happens now, all I do is look that person right in the eyes, smile, and under my breath I say to the spirit of anti-Christ in that person, 'The blood of Christ prevails against you!' I say it just loud enough for the devil in them to hear it. And he hears it and backs off in a hurry. You just try it sometime. Resist the devil, and he will flee from you. He can't stand against the blood of Jesus!"

I wasted no time in trying her technique on my co-worker. It worked, and I never heard another word of hostility out of her. No mention of it was ever made between us, and several months later I was transferred to work in the Intensive Care Unit and forgot the incident.

One day as I was about to get into my car after work, I heard someone call my name. I was startled to look up and see the nurse I had worked with looking earnestly at me. She said nothing except, "I'm sorry, Linda."

"It's alright," I called after her. Driving home, I had to keep wiping the tears from my eyes. I couldn't stop thanking Jesus for working in her heart. Ever since then I have seen time and time again just how powerful the blood of Christ is against persecution.

## Taming The Roaring Lion

One day a friend called me from work and said, "I'm scared I'm going to lose my job today. I don't know what to do." She then told me that her boss had grown increasingly hateful toward her. From the incidents that she quickly told me, I discerned that this was probably another case of demonic persecution. His hostility had no real basis, and the more she tried to show the love of Christ toward him, the more animosity he returned.

On this particular morning he was intensely agitated. He had said to her, "I want to talk to you privately right after lunch." So she called me and, almost in tears, said, "What can I do? I know he's going to fire me, and I need this job."

Quickly I told her the story about the hateful nurse and the woman who told me how to handle persecution. I explained that she must realize her boss was a victim of the devil, who was using him to persecute Christ in her. I told her what to say to that evil spirit in him the next time he started intimidating her. "Call me back after you talk to your boss and let me know how it went," I told her.

That afternoon she called me back and exclaimed, "You won't believe what happened! It was great! When I first went into my boss' office after lunch, he was glaring at me. He started talking real mean, telling me all the things he didn't like about me. But while he was talking, I was doing what you told me to do—keeping calm, I kept saying under my breath, over and over, 'The blood of Christ prevails against you. The blood of Christ prevails against you,' to that evil spirit in him. I was really scared, but I kept saying it.

"Pretty soon I noticed that my boss was lightening up a bit. He stopped scowling and saying mean things, and after a few minutes he even started smiling and telling me the things he *liked* about me and the job I'm doing for him. Then he started telling me just how much he appreciated my efforts—and guess what! By the time I walked out of his office he had actually given me a *raise*!"

To show you how this technique can help you if you are being persecuted by your husband, let me tell you about another friend of mine whose husband was unsaved. She anxiously confided in me one day, "I don't know what to do about my husband. He has become so resentful of my faith lately. The other day I asked him to listen to a child-rearing tape by Dr. Dobson. My husband asked me if Dobson was a Christian, and I said, 'Yes, he is. But that isn't why I'd like you to listen to the tape. I just think he has some good advice for parents that we might use.' My husband's face turned red, and he shoved me against the wall and said, 'I hate Christians! I hate Christians!' It's getting to the point that I'm afraid of my own husband."

I then explained my "secret weapon" and told her, "Love him enough to help him get free from the demonic influence that is tormenting you both. After you try this technique, let me know how things are going."

The next time I talked to her, I asked her if she had tried it out.

"Oh, I sure did!" she said.

I asked how her husband was behaving now.

"Like a pussycat," she smiled. "Like a big, sweet pussycat!"

# 11

# THE JOY OF
# ACCEPTANCE

*"For I have learned to be content in whatever circumstances I am"*—Philippians 4:11.

I spent many unhappy years wishing my husband were a born-again Christian. He disliked my "religion," he disliked my Christian friends, and sometimes I felt that he disliked me. Once I asked him to give me just one good reason for not liking my Christians friends. He thought for a moment and then replied, "They *smile* all the time."

No one could really empathize with my feelings. I felt lonely at church, flanked on either side by my two sons, but no husband. I felt lonely in Sunday school, as one of the few women who never had a husband sitting next to her whom she could admire and feel protected by. I felt lonely when my Christian friends had social gatherings and I was not invited. Church and fellowship were important to me, yet I never felt fully included.

It seemed that all activities catered to couples or the youth, with nothing for wives of unbelievers.

I also felt that others thought I was not a good church member because I missed many activities and rarely volunteered for service; but I couldn't risk upsetting my husband by becoming too involved in church functions. Sunday morning worship and the ladies' daytime Bible studies were all I dared attend, and even then I felt alone.

## Waiting For Happiness

At age twenty, I walked the few blocks from our college student apartment complex to a neighborhood church with my son's tiny hand in mine. A few years later I was packing him and the new baby in and out of the car with diaper bags and punkin seat for the drive to church from our new city apartment. As the little boys sitting beside me in church grew over the years, so did my discontent. Instead of growing more used to being alone, I became increasingly unhappy about it. The feeling, "Why can't I have a Christian husband like all my friends?" became more intense and painful with time.

I began to torture myself: "If only my husband would go to church with me." "If only he were less critical of my commitment to the Lord." "If only he were more like Mary's husband, who teaches Sunday school." "If only he would help me raise the boys as Christians."

These thoughts gnawed at me constantly. I knew I could never be truly happy until all of those "if onlys" came true. So, day after day, year after year, I waited for my husband to get saved so I could be happy. I lived with deferred happiness while I carried around that deep-inside, wishful ache. Sometimes the ache was unbearably painful. Sometimes it lurked just beneath the surface of my consciousness. But it was always there, throbbing.

Then I read Hanna Hurnard's lovely book, *Hind's Feet On High Places* (Living Books). The unhappy little "Much Afraid" was led into a great, sandy desert by the "Chief Shepherd." She never saw a living thing there until one day, under a tiny leak in a water pipe, she discovered a small, golden flower blooming happily, all alone. When "Much-Afraid" asked its name, the flower replied, "Behold me! My name is Acceptance-with-Joy!"

I, too, eventually learned the secret of acceptance with joy in the midst of my desert experience. I'm sure it was born not so much out of Christian maturity as human desperation. I was sick of being miserable. Something inside me said, "Enough already! I'm tired of waiting to be happy. If my husband doesn't get saved until he is ninety-nine years old, just look at all the years I will have wasted being miserable about it. This is my life, and I'm not going to waste any more of it being unhappy about something I have no power to change. I'm just going to have to accept what I can't change and be happy in spite of it!"

I finally realized the absurdity of living with the attitude, "Someday my husband will get saved, and *then* I'll be happy." It finally dawned on me that life is not made up of "somedays" but of thousands of "todays." If I wanted to enjoy my life—ever—I had to enjoy it and be happy *today*—regardless of circumstances and no matter what my husband's spiritual condition. I had prayed and believed that eventually he would be saved because God always answers our prayers. But no longer could I put my life on "hold" waiting for that day. I had to accept, totally, the fact that my husband was not a believer and live with it happily.

No more being forlorn in church; no more wishfully picturing my husband at my side; and no more thinking of myself as an inferior Christian. I began to hold my head high and prove to the world that a woman is no less of a person because she is alone—not even in church. She is not half of a pair: she is *complete in Christ*.

I became determined to walk in the joy of the Lord rather than the world's "happiness," which is based on circumstances. The more I sought my contentment in Jesus in spite of my feelings, the more real joy I experienced and the less circumstances mattered.

So, if I thought those women at church with a man by their side looked smart and serene, I would look more so. If they could reflect the joy of the Lord sitting beside their husbands, I could reflect His joy sitting alone. When I saw a woman walking tall next to her husband in church, I walked taller. Christ alone would be enough for me. And the more I acted that way, the more I felt that way. The more I accepted myself totally as the wife of an unbeliever, the more I felt accepted by others. I began to feel much better about myself as a person.

## Freedom In Christ

As I felt better about myself away from home, a funny thing happened. I started feeling better about myself at home, too. I stopped being overly concerned about my husband's disapproval of my faith. Instead, I took on the attitude of, "Look, we are both adults, free to make our own choices. You don't choose to be a Christian at this time— fine. I accept that, and I can love you just as you are. But I have chosen to follow the Lord Jesus Christ, and *you* must learn to accept that. If you truly love me, you will have to love me just the way I am, too.

"You don't lose any sleep worrying about whether I approve of your beliefs, your friends, or your behavior. Fine, I accept that. But no longer am I going to be miserable over your reaction to mine. You will have to accept my beliefs, friends, and behavior as part of me.

"You are free to live as you choose—as an unbeliever. But I must also be free to live as I choose—as a Christian wife who loves and respects you but who is also true to her faith. We must accept each other exactly as we are, with unconditional love and kindness.''

This is not something I ever said out loud to my husband. If I had spoken it, he would have considered it another meaningless emotional speech. Instead, I just made it the attitude of my heart and lived it. That spoke louder than words.

After that, I began to experience total acceptance of my husband for the first time. No more trying to change him or coerce him into anything. No more disappointment when he acted stubborn. No more misgiving looks or sad sighs of resignation from me. I would just think, You aren't interested in the Lord? Fine. I can accept that. I love you anyway. And at last my husband was free to be himself and experience life however he chose—whatever the consequences—free of pressure from me. I only expected that he treat me with the same respect.

Quickly, I began gaining confidence and total acceptance of myself as a wife. No longer did I feel embarrassed or intimidated about my faith in front of my husband. No more wilting under his disapproving looks. No more guilt. I was a Christian and unashamed of it. I didn't flaunt it, but neither did I act apologetically. I followed the orders in 1 Peter 3:14: "But even if you should suffer for the sake of righteousness, you are blessed. And do not fear their intimidation, and do not be troubled."

I began to respect my right to be true to myself, to be who I really was, and to feel the same way toward my husband. Someday he would change, but today I would allow him the freedom to be whatever he wanted to be. No longer living in "Someday Land," I was living totally in the present. I turned "someday" over to the Lord to worry about. He in turn give me "today," and I received it with joy.

After that it was easy to let cynical remarks that used to bring me to tears slide off me like water off a duck's feathers. I'd just shrug things off with, "That's the way you feel, but I don't. I respect your right to disagree."

This change in my attitude seemed to be a bit disconcerting to my husband at first. He was used to seeing me act the role of the downtrodden martyr at the whim of his sarcastic remarks. When I acted like I no longer cared, perhaps he thought I no longer cared about him. But I still acted consistently kind and loving while remaining unruffled. Soon it was obvious to him that I would not let myself be manipulated by my emotions anymore. When he saw there was no point in being difficult, he stopped being so abrasive. By accepting circumstances the way they were, I had inadvertently diffused a point of contention between us, and our relationship improved greatly.

Today I sit next to my husband in church just like I always dreamed of doing. We have a whole new relationship based on oneness in Christ.

It was a long, strenuous road from walking to church with my toddler to the place where we are today. But it was well worth the trip.

I can't say that my discovering the secret of acceptance caused my husband to become a Christian any sooner than if I hadn't, but I wouldn't be surprised. I can say that it made the trip a lot smoother.

# 12

# PRACTICING PERSISTENCE

*"And having done everything ... stand firm"*—Ephesians 6:13.

Some things in life only come through persistent effort, and your husband's salvation may well be one of those things. You may have to weather many a marital storm and stand against many spiritual attacks before your husband becomes a Christian. But if you stand firm in your faith in God and back up that faith with your actions, God will do everything in His power to keep you from being disappointed.

If I have learned anything in my twenty years as a Christian, it is this: You cannot be more faithful to God than He will be to you in return. God will not be beholding to His children. Whatever you offer up to Him in faith, He will return to you tenfold. That is why the law of tithing works. You can't outgive God.

Galatians 6:7-9 states,

> Do not be deceived, God is not mocked; for whatever a man sows, this he will also reap. For the one who sows to his own flesh shall from the flesh reap corruption, but the one who sows to the Spirit shall from the Spirit reap eternal life. And let us not lose heart in doing good, for in due time we shall reap if we do not grow weary.

If you sow the seed of tithing, you will reap financial abundance. If you sow the seed of the flesh, you will reap corruption. If you sow the seed of the Spirit, you will reap eternal life. Likewise, if you sow the seed of persistent faith in prayer, God will see to it that you reap accordingly.

In Mark 11:24, Jesus said, "Therefore I say to you, all things for which you pray and ask, believe that you have received them, and they shall be granted you."

Do you want a husband who cherishes you? Then sow seeds of respect for him. A man who receives respect from his wife will, in return, cherish her. (See Chapter 4.)

Do you want a husband who loves the Lord with all his heart? Then sow seeds of loving your husband and being a Christian example that he can be proud of.

Do you want God to save your husband? Then sow seeds of faith by believing that God will do it.

Stop speaking words of unbelief such as, "My husband is a hopeless case; he will never get saved." Speak words of faith such as, "*When* my husband gets saved . . ." instead of, "*If* my husband gets saved." "*If*" implies doubt. "*When*" implies faith. Be persistent in your faith, even with the words you speak.

## Never Give Up

Persistence is the key. It means "patience, perseverance, determination, steadfastness, resolution, firmness, tenacity, stamina, stick-to-itiveness, diligence, and tirelessness." In short, persistence means *never giving up*.

Sound like a tall order? Perhaps. But your goal is worthy of it. And the fruit of the Spirit will supply all the characteristics you need to be persistent. You need only supply some rugged determination.

Just as Jacob wrestled with the angel until he received the blessing that he wanted, wives of unbelievers must cling to God with all their might until they receive what they want most—their husband's salvation. Get a firm grip on God, and don't let go no matter how tough or painful things get. Insist that you won't let go until you win.

Do you know that the only way a Christian can lose a spiritual battle is to give up and quit?

It's the *only way.* Do you know what makes Christians give up? They believe the "father of lies" rather than their Father in heaven! Satan will tell you, "There is no hope for your husband. You might as well give up. Divorce him. He will never change." But our Father in heaven says, "With God all things are possible" (Matthew 19:26).

Satan's lies can only come true if you believe them. Proverbs 23:7 says, "For as he thinks within himself, so he is." If you think you're a loser, you are! If you think you're a winner, you are! The winner is the one who won't quit until she wins.

I know a woman named Pat who refused to quit believing for her husband's salvation for over twenty years. Even after her husband was diagnosed with terminal cancer, she kept believing. His physical condition deteriorated month by month, yet she persisted in faith that God would save him. She spent hours in prayer, until one day the Lord said to her, "I'll leave no stone unturned, but it is your husband's decision."

Pat kept praying and believing God could do it. She knew only a rare heart can resist such conviction. Finally, one week before he died, her husband said to her, "I received Jesus as my Lord."

Twenty years of persistence had produced a fruitful harvest—Pat's husband was snatched out of eternal death into eternal life.

Another woman, whom I'll call Jenny, persisted in faith after many years of marriage to a man who was often unfaithful to her. After learning that her husband was having yet another affair, Jenny could take no more and filed for divorce on the biblical grounds of adultery. But she said, "I may not be around to see the day, but I still believe that my husband will become a Christian. There have been too many prayers sent up on his behalf to fail. I know God will save him, and I trust that He will reward all my years of faithfulness by giving me a godly husband in his place."

She was absolutely right. A few months later she was remarried in a touching church ceremony to an eager new Christian. Who was he? Her newly converted husband, of course!

## Obedience To Number One

There have been times when women who were persistent in faith and obedience to God had to choose between obeying God's Word or directly opposing orders from their husbands. A good example of this was Polly Wigglesworth, the wife of the then backslidden Smith Wigglesworth.

Obedient to the scriptural admonition of "not forsaking our own assembling together" (Hebrews 10:25), she went to a church meeting one night despite Smith's objections. But Polly was not the type of wife to use Scripture to flaunt her husband's authority and insist on her own way.

When she got home that night, Smith had locked her out of the house, forcing Polly to sleep leaning against the door in the vestibule. To show her respect for her husband, the next morning she lovingly prepared Smith's favorite breakfast. Later, Smith testified that this incident caused him to return to the Lord. He subsequently became one of the greatest evangelists in history.

A word of caution: never disobey your husband unless you know beyond the shadow of a doubt that you must do it to obey the Lord. Sometimes a woman must be obedient to her highest authority, the Lord, at the expense of obedience to her second-in-command, her husband.

This should never be done without great forethought and prayer. Polly Wigglesworth may have missed many a church meeting until that one fateful night when she sensed that God was telling her to go. But if her disobedience to Smith that night had caused him to abandon her and their children, she would have been very regretful if she had not been sure she had heard God's voice. That would have been a difficult time for second thoughts. Unless God has specifically told you to disobey your husband, don't do it.

Often a marriage is saved even in spite of such adversity. But I believe it is foolish to insist that a woman stay with a husband who is threatening her life with beatings or adultery (A.I.D.S. or other venereal disease being quite possible as a result). Neither do I think God wants children to suffer permanent physical and/or consequential emotional scars from an abusive husband. I believe God has good, common sense, don't you? I wish

Christians would have the same. The Lord desires compassion from His Church, not dogged legalism.

In spite of all the problems an unequally yoked union can bring, I believe that the great majority of marriages can be saved and conformed to God's will through the wife's persistent faith and obedience to God.

"Now he who plants and he who waters are one; but each will receive his own reward according to his own labor" (1 Corinthians 3:8).

Keep planting those seeds of persistence.

# 13

# THE PROVERBS 31 WOMAN

*"An excellent wife, who can find? For her worth is far above jewels. The heart of her husband trusts in her, and he will have no lack of gain. She does him good and not evil all the days of her life"*—Proverbs 31:10-12.

This Proverbs 31 woman is my favorite role model. I read verses ten through thirty-one more than any others in the Bible. There I find inspiration, renewal, and a constant reminder of my goals as a woman, wife, and mother.

Over the years, as I have tried to conform to her example, I have gradually seen the benefits and rewards of being a Proverbs 31 woman unfolding in my own life. And I am looking forward to that day when I, too, experience the gratitude and compliments that she did in verses 28-29: "Her children rise up and bless her; her husband also, and he praises her, saying, 'Many daughters have done nobly, but you excel them all.'"

Next to my Lord's "Well done good and faithful servant" (Matthew 25:23), those are the words I want most to hear at the end of my life.

## Works Of Love

Some women complain, "I get exhausted just reading everything that the Proverbs 31 woman did. How on earth could I ever do all that?" What they don't realize is that her accomplishments were not all done in one day. I am sure that these verses tell the story of a godly woman's entire marriage, with all the various times and seasons a woman experiences as she and her family grow older.

When her children were young, she probably kept busy with cooking, weaving, making clothing for her family, and other domestic duties, as noted in verses 13, 14, 15, 19, and 21:

"She looks for wool and flax, and works with her hands in delight."

"She is like merchant ships; she brings her food from afar."

"She rises also while it is still night, and gives food to her household, and portions to her maidens."

"She stretches out her hands to the distaff, and her hands grasp the spindle."

"She is not afraid of the snow for her household, for all her household are clothed with scarlet."

Then, as the children grew older, she probably applied her sewing skills to a home-based business. "She makes linen garments and sells them, and supplies belts to the tradesmen" (verse 24).

Later, perhaps she took her savings from her sewing trade and invested it into her next business venture. "She considers a field and buys it; from her earnings she plants a vineyard" (verse 16).

The Proverbs 31 woman not only worked hard but maintained quality of character. "She opens her mouth in wisdom, and the teaching of kindness is on her tongue" (verse 26).

She was active in ministry as the needs arose. "She extends her hand to the poor; and she stretches out her hands to the needy" (verse 20).

She also kept physically fit. "She girds herself with strength, and makes her arms strong" (verse 17).

Her faith in God gave her a bright outlook on the future. "Strength and dignity are her clothing, and she smiles at the future" (verse 25).

She dressed well. "She makes coverings for herself; her clothing is fine linen and purple" (verse 22). She wasn't the type to run around in a ratty housecoat and curlers. *Her* husband looked forward to coming home at the end of the day.

And, of course, she was never lazy. "She senses that her gain is good; her lamp does not go out at night" (verse 18). I can't imagine her wasting time on those horrid soap operas. "She looks well to the ways of her household, and does not eat

111

the bread of idleness'' (verse 27). *That's* the kind of bread that really makes you fat!

## Commitment To The Family

Notice that even though she was an industrious woman, the Proverbs 31 woman also had "maidens," or servants, as noted in verse fifteen. At one time, I thought that hiring help would be a sign of my personal inadequacy as a wife. But after noticing that she had help, I knew it must be okay. There have been times since then—when I was working a forty-hour, away-from-home job—that having someone come in once a week to clean the house meant the difference between my total exhaustion and having time to spend with my family.

Any woman who tries to be "superwoman" and takes on too much at one time is cheating herself and her family. You just can't do everything. If you need hired help and can afford it, by all means get it in good conscience.

The most important thing to note about the Proverbs 31 woman is that she never did anything at the expense of neglecting her family. That's the "barometer" I use to measure whether I am taking on more than the Lord has asked of me. If my family is seeing too little of me, or my home is becoming too disorganized, I know that it's time to stop everything and reevaluate my priorities.

Also, if I am chronically "tired and crabby," I know that my circuits are being overloaded and it's time to back off.

At a recent parents' meeting, I raised my hand in response to a request for volunteers for a certain school project. My husband looked at me out of the corner of his eye and whispered, "Put that hand down *right now*!" I took that as divine guidance to pass on that project.

In the past, I have resigned from good jobs for one or more of the above reasons and never regretted it. What does it pay to gain the world and have your family life falling apart at the seams? God eventually provides for my heart's desires if I am faithful to put family responsibilities ahead of my lust for new carpeting or the latest appliance.

Keeping myself fully active, rather than wasting time on endless neighborhood gossip sessions or television quiz shows, is the secret to a happy, prosperous home. A woman doesn't have to bring home a paycheck to prosper her home. She can save hundreds of dollars by taking the time to be a wise and frugal shopper, cooking healthful meals that keep her family out of the doctor's office, and sewing or mending clothing, among other things.

### Sensible Schedules

Whether working at an outside job or full time at home, a woman does need a schedule, just as much as a family needs a financial budget.

A work schedule is really a time budget. It helps you see what needs to be done and when you can do it, without feeling overwhelmed. My schedule can be changed as the week's events unfold; but I try to stick to it because when I do I feel less pressured and have a great sense of satisfaction at the end of the week. Right now my schedule looks like this:

Sunday: Church and family day
Monday: Clean the kitchen and baths
Tuesday: Vacuum and dust the house
Wednesday: Laundry and ironing
Thursday: Grocery shopping and errands
Friday: My free day
Saturday: Outdoor work

This schedule only requires a couple of hours a day and is my key to freedom. It leaves time for other work and interests yet keeps my home in good working order. I never have to do any special cleaning for company because there is never more than a week's worth of dirt at any one time, which is an acceptable level to me. Cleaning the house at the beginning of the week lets me enjoy it a few days until it is "destroyed" over the weekend. I fit in the extra jobs, such as washing the windows, whenever the mood hits me and I have the extra time. It's a loose schedule, but it works for me. If my lifestyle changes later, I'll adjust my schedule accordingly.

If there is no rhyme or reason to your weekly schedule, why not make one to fit your lifestyle? If you don't think you have time to fit everything into a schedule, you probably need one most of all. Write down everything that realistically needs to be done every week, then divide it into days and time slots that fit your way of life.

You may find that you have been wasting hours every week that can be put to better use. Or you may have to sit down with your husband and children and say, "All these things have to be done, and I can't do them all, as you can see. I need your help." Then give *them* a schedule, too. Remember, even the Proverbs 31 woman had help.

## Praise In The Gates

I love and admire the Proverbs 31 woman so much that sometimes I wish the Lord had seen fit to tell us her name. But in His wisdom He did not, perhaps because He wants her name to be yours and mine. Try reading through those verses while inserting your own name wherever you see the word "she." Doesn't that sound great?

My favorite verse in Proverbs 31 is verse twenty-three: "Her husband is known in the gates, when he sits among the elders of the land." In those days, community leaders met at the main entrance to the city to discuss politics, religion, or business. If your husband is not yet an "elder in the land," begin now, in faith, to envision him as one.

Treat him as if he is already a great leader respected by your church and community. Then behave as if you were already the esteemed wife of such an admired man. After seeing himself as such every day in the reflection of your eyes, chances are that it won't be long until he is all that and more.

Verses thirty and thirty-one say, "Charm is deceitful and beauty is vain, but a woman who fears the Lord, she shall be praised. Give her the product of her hands, and let her works praise her in the gates."

Your husband will surely be the one praising you in the gates.

# 14
# WHO'S THE GREATEST?

*"Thou hast also given me the shield of Thy salvation, and Thy hand upholds me; and Thy gentleness makes me great"*—Psalm 18:35.

Do you sometimes wish you could be more useful and important to the church like the women who have Christian husbands? Have you ever envied those wives whose husbands allow them to serve Jesus to their hearts' desire? Do you compare yourself to those women and come up short? I often did.

Why is it that wives of believing men are so useful to the Lord, anyway? Do they have something that you lack? Are they better Christians? Why do they have great ministries while you watch from the sidelines?

Just for fun, I'd like you to do a little assignment. Get a pen and paper, and make a list of all the women you know at your church, from the most important to the least important. Who at your church serves Jesus best? Put her name at the top. Who do you think is the most useful and dependable or spends the most time serving others for Christ? Whom do you admire and most wish to emulate? List them all, and don't read any further until you are finished.

Now let's go over your list together and see what makes these particular women so important to the church.

May I take a guess at who is first on your list? Could it be the pastor's wife? How did I guess? Easy—everyone knows how important the pastor's wife is. She has to be very dedicated to the Lord and her husband to be a helpmeet and role model for the entire Body of Christ. A pastor's wife lives her life in a goldfish bowl for all to observe. You made an excellent selection in choosing her. She's a terrific lady.

And who is number two on your list? I bet she's the leader of your Bible study group, right? Perfect choice. What a gift she has for bringing the Word of God to life and making it a practical help for everyday living. Where would we be without women like her?

You don't have to sell me on your third choice. Yes, the president of the ladies' circle is quite a worker. She must spend endless hours planning and conducting meetings and luncheons, and she always looks so stunning, doesn't she? I've always admired women like her who can handle the limelight so well.

Who else do you have on your list? Let's see, there's your spiritual mother and confidante—good. And a little further down the list is the dear sister who teaches your children in Sunday school. Thank the Lord for her! And I see you haven't forgotten the church secretary. She handles so many details with such poise. Very good.

But . . . I hate to say this. I'm wondering, dear, where is *your* name on the list? I can't seem to find—oh, there it is! I thought for a moment that you left yourself out. But your name is down near the bottom, scrunched in between the lady that waters the plants in the church vestibule and the third alternate Sunday school bus driver.

I realize you can only do so much since your husband isn't saved. Sure, you help out with Vacation Bible School one week every summer, and you fill in once in a while as a substitute Sunday school teacher when someone forgets to show up. No big deal. You'd do a lot more if you could, but I know how it is when your husband isn't saved. He just won't allow any of that church business on *his* time, right?

So there you sit in your rightful place at the bottom, wishing with all your might that you could be a bit higher up on the list of those serving the Lord. Maybe someday (when you're an elderly widow) you can give more time to Jesus. In the meantime, you feel embarrassed and unimportant, hoping the Lord, at least, understands.

119

You carry on with your appointed tasks at home—uninteresting, unfulfilling, and unimportant. At times you feel almost *un-Christian*.

## Lordship And Humility

Once Jesus was asked to decide which of His disciples He considered most important. A dispute was going on in their ranks, so James' and John's mother, Mrs. Zebedee, decided to get it settled once and for all. She knew her sons were the obvious best choices for Top Banana in Jesus' future Kingdom, and she made it her business to tell Him so.

"Command that in Your kingdom these two sons of mine may sit, one on Your right and one on Your left," she demanded (Matthew 20:21).

"You do not know what you are asking for," replied Jesus as He turned His eyes upon James and John, who were standing eagerly behind their mother. "Are you able to drink the cup that I am about to drink?" He asked them (verse 22).

"We are able," they answered enthusiastically, not knowing that it was an excruciating, bloody cup of which Jesus was speaking.

"My cup you shall drink," He promised, foretelling their future martyrdom, "but to sit on My right and on My left, this is not Mine to give, but it is for those for whom it has been prepared by My Father" (verse 23).

Then Jesus turned abruptly toward the other disciples, who were indignantly vying for equal consideration in this sudden outbreak of one-upmanship. His eyes darkened as He looked at each of them, one by one. Jesus realized that He must get this lesson across to them in the short time left, or His earthly mission would be a dismal failure in spite of His great sacrifice. On the night before His crucifixion He would show them a profound example when, wearing only a towel, He would tenderly bathe their feet with His own hands.

His arm swept toward Jerusalem as He cried, "You know that the rulers of the Gentiles lord it over them, and their great men exercise authority over them" (verse 25).

Then the Lord's tone of voice lowered as He deliberately measured His words:

> "It is not so among you, but whoever wishes to become great among you shall be your servant, and whoever wishes to be first among you shall be your slave; just as the Son of Man did not come to be served, but to serve, and to give His life as a ransom for many"—verses 26-28.

The disciples looked questioningly at one another. What kind of statement was this? It was as strange as when their Master had said, "But many who are first, will be last; and the last, first" (Mark 10:31).

They did not understand. And they would not understand, really, until after they witnessed His shocking death on a cross. Only then would they understand the price of greatness.

Which brings me back to you, dear Sister. Who do you think pays a greater price to follow Jesus today? Is it your pastor's wife, who serves Jesus alongside her husband? Or could it be *you,* who must serve Jesus alone, perhaps in spite of your husband's opposition? Is it the president of the Ladies' Circle, who receives recognition and praise from the women she serves? Or could it be you, who serves an unsaved, unappreciative husband in spite of an often unsupportive church?

Whom do you think Jesus would most highly commend—the woman who is gifted with teaching God's Word in a Bible study or the woman who seeks out and clings to every word of truth in order to survive a difficult home situation? Would Jesus think any more of the mature spiritual counsellor than He would of the woman who needs and humbly receives that counsel, treasuring God's wisdom in her heart and applying it to daily circumstances? Who impressed Jesus the most with their giving, the wealthy who gave out of their abundance or the widow who offered God her tiny mite? (See Mark 12:42.) Are you ashamed of your "tiny mites"?

# The Shepherd's Voice

As you proceed down your list of important women, do you see anyone who has a more important role to fill in your own family's needs? Do you see anyone who would exchange places with you if she knew the difficulty you routinely encounter in balancing your priorities between the Lord whom you love and the unbelieving husband whom you also love? Or do you think any of those important women would trade their prestigious spiritual roles for your humble role? Whose role is really the most difficult? Whose requires the greatest dependence on God? Whose is the most needed? And whose, do you think, is really the most important?

It is well and good that we love and appreciate each woman you have listed. They deserve every ounce of credit for being faithful in the positions the Lord has given them. I am sure the Lord is well pleased with them.

But do you really think, my friend, that He could possibly be any less pleased with you? Or have you been deceived into thinking that you, as the wife of an unbeliever, are a second-class citizen in God's Kingdom? If so, maybe you are listening to the wrong voices.

Jesus said, "My sheep hear My voice, and I know them, and they follow Me" (John 10:27). Are you listening to those who can't comprehend the kind of ministry Jesus has called you to because they have never experienced it? Are you listening to the voices of those who are only impressed by "spiritual" things done in front of other "spiritual" people? Are you listening to the voice of the Deceiver? Are you listening to your own self-doubt?

Determine to listen from now on only to the gentle voice of our Shepherd, who says, "If anyone serves Me, let him follow Me; and where I am, there shall my servant also be; if anyone serves Me, the Father will honor him" (John 12:26).

As you serve Christ now in your home by serving your husband, you can rest assured that in due time you will receive great honor—not from men but from the Father, Himself, who says,

> "Well done, thou good and faithful servant: thou hast been faithful over a few things, I will make thee ruler over many things: enter thou into the joy of thy Lord" (Matthew 25:21 *KJV*).

Not until that day of rewards in heaven will anyone know who truly is the greatest among the saints. I am sure that will be a day of many surprises. But I won't be a bit surprised if one of the saints selected for top honors is none other than *you.*

# 15

# TRUE SUBMISSION

*"Wives, submit yourselves unto your own husbands, as it is fit in the Lord"*—Colossians 3:18 KJV.

The wife of an unbeliever often feels caught in that precarious spot "between a rock and a hard place." Submitting to her husband while maintaining a Christian lifestyle is no easy task. Although she wants to obey her spouse in all things, she may often have reservations about what he is asking her to do or the manner in which he is asking.

And woe to her if the only scripture her husband knows is the one quoted above. He then may feel justified in testing her obedience both to himself and God by demanding immediate subservience to his every whim. As a result, the wife feels trapped and resentful.

One friend confided in me, "My husband doesn't obey a thing in the Bible, but he insists that I obey him as the head of the house because the Bible says so. I get so sick of his barking orders at me like a king to a peasant that I finally say, 'Stuff it!' Then I feel guilty. With a wife like me for an example, I can't blame him for not wanting to be a Christian.''

Her husband's limited understanding of God's Word led him to think that marriage is supposed to be a "dictator-doormat" relationship. This left his wife wondering what could be wrong with her to resent such treatment.

## Marriage And The Church

Satan loves to distort Scripture so he can use it to curse us. God intended Scripture to bless us! Satan likes us to have a "Smorgasbord Bible"— picking out what we like and leaving the rest. But to interpret any passage of Scripture correctly, it must be taken in the context of the whole Bible. When the "submission" verses are taken out of context, they can distort God's intended balance in the marriage relationship and be used to make a wife a slave-object. Ephesians 5:22-33 says,

> Wives, be subject to your own husbands, as to the Lord. For the husband is the head of the wife, as Christ also is the head of the church, He Himself being the Savior of the body. But as the church is subject to Christ, so also the wives ought to be to their husbands in

everything. Husbands, love your wives, just as Christ also loved the church and gave Himself up for her; that He might sanctify her, having cleansed her by the washing of water with the word, that He might present to Himself the church in all her glory, having no spot or wrinkle or any such thing; but that she should be holy and blameless. So husbands ought also to love their own wives as their own bodies. He who loves his own wife loves himself; for no one ever hated his own flesh, but nourishes and cherishes it, just as Christ also does the church, because we are members of His body. For this cause a man shall leave his father and mother, and shall cleave to his wife; and the two shall become one flesh. This mystery is great; but I am speaking with reference to Christ and the church. Nevertheless let each individual among you also love his own wife even as himself; and let the wife see to it that she respect her husband.

As you can see, God designed marriage to be a loving, giving relationship between two self-sacrificing adults. Marriage is intended to be a picture of Christ (the husband) giving Himself to the Church (the wife) and the Church serving Christ. The picture is marred, however, if one partner does all the taking while insisting the other partner do all the giving. Such imbalance destroys the reflection of Christ and the Church, and the Lord is not glorified on the earth.

The world cannot see a reflection of the Church if a husband treats his wife lovingly while she, in return, acts like a selfish shrew. Nor can the world see a reflection of Christ if the wife is slavishly submitting to a tyrant. In either extreme, God's desired balance is destroyed along with the beauty of the marriage relationship.

Hopefully, the unequally yoked wife does not act like a selfish shrew; a Christ-centered attitude would not allow such egocentric behavior. Self and Christ cannot sit on the throne of one's heart simultaneously.

## The Martyr Complex

A more common imbalance in the unequally yoked marriage is the type of situation that my friend complained about: When the husband, in rebellion against God's Word, uses that same Word to whip his wife into submission.

All too often such a wife thinks she can only please God by indulging her husband in his tyranny and obeying his every command, no matter how cruel or unscriptural. But by playing the part of "Edith" to her "Archie Bunker," she is only creating a monster who secretly loathes his own selfishness and his wife's lack of self-esteem.

Such women fail to see that the Lord has not called wives to be martyrs. God doesn't make martyrs, the devil does. Satan stoned Stephen to death, not the Lord. God would rather see a saint be martyred than to deny Christ, but in a marriage that should not be necessary. Satan comes to steal, kill, and destroy. Jesus comes that we might have life and have it abundantly. (See John 10:10.) God has called us to be whole and victorious, not broken and downtrodden. If you are setting yourself up to be a martyr, you are cooperating with Satan.

A martyr says, "Let me lie down, darling, so it will be easier for you to walk on me." A truly victorious saint says, "I am sorry, but I cannot get drunk or use drugs with you. That is something you will have to do without me."

If my words seem harsh, perhaps that's because this is a reformed martyr speaking. At one time, early in my Christian walk, I thought I had to go along with my husband no matter what he asked me to do. Believe it or not, that was the popular teaching of the day in the church. Preachers naively thought that if a woman trusted God, He would not let her husband tell her to do anything against His will. Supposedly, if a wife obeyed her husband in everything, eventually that would bring him to Christ.

My husband's reaction was quite the opposite. The effect it had on me was not good, either, since we went to bars and wild parties with people who I think would have been right at home in Sodom.

I finally decided that neither Mark nor I were enjoying each other's company at these events; if my husband wanted to continue going, it would not be with my blessing. By accompanying him, I felt I was saying, "It's okay with me if you go to these places, as long as you take me, too." If I had continued going along, I would have been in danger of becoming like the people who made me so uncomfortable. Playing the part of the martyr can lead to compromising, hypocritical positions.

Women have a tendency to allow themselves a martyr mentality because they have picked up the idea that the male sex is superior to the female. But a woman's common sense should tell her that is foolish.

Some people think men are superior to women because God created the man first. Have you ever "created" anything with your hands? Which product came out better, your first attempt, or your second? That may seem funny, but it shows the absurdity of that argument.

The Bible refers to the woman as the "weaker vessel." But that simply refers to physical weakness. It's a biological fact that men are physically stronger than women. But would you rather be stronger physically or stronger inwardly? Studies have proven that the female (a product of two "X" chromosomes) is genetically stronger than the male (a weaker combination of one "X" and one "Y" chromosome). As a result, more female infants survive the first year of life than males, and women have greater endurance. I think God knew that women would need more endurance!

I would like you to ponder one more point: of the two roles, male and female, which do you really think requires the most flexibility, diplomacy, and intuitive wisdom? Do you think God would give that role to the "inferior" sex?

## A Matter Of Choice

To achieve balance in your role as a wife, it might be helpful to imagine a child's see-saw. One end of the see-saw is marked "slave." The other end is marked "self." If you go too far in either extreme your marriage will be out of balance. Where do you achieve perfect balance? Right in the center, which is marked "servant."

The chasm between "self" and "servant" is vast and obvious. "Self" serves self, while "servant" serves others. They are opposites.

The difference between "slave" and "servant" is more subtle. Both serve others. But there is a word with which one can quickly differentiate between "slave" and "servant." That word is *choice.*

A slave serves others because she has no choice. She is compelled, and there is no way out. A servant, however, chooses to serve. No one forces her to, and she is free to walk away at any time.

Therefore, a servant is more appreciated, receives better treatment, and has better self-esteem than a slave.

The matter of choice makes as much difference in a woman's submission as water differs from ice. Both have the same chemical composition—but what a different effect! If you find yourself as cool as a popsicle when the lights are turned out at night, chances are that you feel you have no choices in your marriage.

Jesus Christ came to the earth to be "the servant of all," not a slave. He made it clear to all who were attempting to kill Him that He had *chosen* to be where He was. Many people have the mistaken idea that Jesus was a weakling who got crucified against His will. But Jesus made it absolutely clear that no one could *take* His life against His will.

When the chief priests and elders swarmed upon Him with swords and clubs in the Garden of Gethsemane, Jesus said to them, "Do you think that I cannot appeal to My Father, and He will at once put at My disposal more than twelve legions of angels?" (Matthew 26:53). He was letting them know they could not take Him against His will.

In John 10:17-18, Jesus infuriated the Jews by saying,

> "For this reason the Father loves Me, because I lay down My life that I may take it again. No one has taken it away

from Me, but I lay it down on My own initiative. I have authority to lay it down, and I have authority to take it up again. This commandment I received from My Father."

Jesus' words were proven true on the cross: "He said, 'It is finished!' And He bowed His head, and gave up His Spirit" (John 19:30).

Jesus' life was not taken from Him; He gave it freely. At other times, such as in the fourth chapter of Luke, Jesus simply walked away from those who tried to throw Him off a cliff. He didn't always do what others wanted. Jesus said,

"Truly, truly, I say to you, the Son can do nothing of Himself, unless it is something He sees the Father doing; for whatever the Father does, these things the Son also does in like manner."

"I can do nothing on My own initiative."

"For I have come down from heaven, not to do My own will, but the will of Him who sent Me."

"And He who sent Me is with Me; He has not left Me alone, for I always do the things that are pleasing to Him"—John 5:19,30; 6:38; 8:29.

Jesus always did what His Father wanted.

It was Christ's self-sacrifice for His Bride that won His authority as the Head of the Church. God still requires that same self-sacrifice today of men who wish to exercise authority as the head of their wives.

Tom Sine, in his book *The Mustard Seed Conspiracy,* states,

> "Many Christians have been taught that Paul's teaching on headship is a biblical basis for a male-dominated, authoritarian chain-of-command system. However, a growing number of biblical scholars insist that the word 'headship' in the Greek doesn't have anything to do with authority over anyone else—man, woman, or child. It means 'life source.' Christ is the head of the church because he is its Savior; he 'loved the church and gave himself up for her' (Ephesians 5:25, *RSV*). As head he also nurtures her growth (Ephesians 4:15-16). This, then, must be the meaning of male headship: self-giving, nurturing love rather than autocratic rule.
>
> "Jesus himself never ordered people around or pulled rank. Instead, he invited. He taught. He loved. He nurtured. He served. He trusted the

Spirit of God to guide people's behavior. In the New Testament we don't see Jesus ordering his disciples around like a top sergeant. We see him washing their feet.''

A wife who has the attitude, ''If you don't love me as Christ loved the Church and gave Himself up for her, then I'm not going to submit to you,'' is just as wrong as the wife who plays the part of the doormat-martyr. Someone has to be the first one to give themselves for the other. One partner has to lay down pride and self first. Either the husband or the wife has to be the servant for a while, teaching by example what it means to give of self. Who is better qualified to do this than the one who knows Jesus Christ, the servant of all, best?

A wife's healthy, non-self-deprecating attitude of freely giving and freely serving brings fulfillment to herself and her marriage. Only then can she be a Christlike servant. Only then can she say, ''I am not submitting to you because you demand it or because I must. I am submitting to you because I choose to, because I love you, and because it is pleasing to the Father.''

This is true submission.

# 16

# AN HONORABLE CALLING

*"To every thing there is a season, and a time to every purpose under the heaven"*—Ecclesiastes 3:1 *KJV.*

It is time for the Body of Christ to realize that the Christian wife of an unbeliever is not a second-class citizen in the Church. She is a woman whom God has called to a noble and difficult ministry. Wives of unbelievers must stop regarding themselves as failures incapable of getting their husbands saved and instead see themselves as selected saints chosen to represent Christ to their husbands in the most intimate of relationships—marriage. And it is time for us all to acknowledge that being the wife of an unsaved husband is not a sin but, in fact, an honorable calling.

That calling is honorable regardless of the consequences. It doesn't matter whether or not her husband eventually becomes a Christian. Even if he never does, she should experience no shame.

In fact, the longer her husband remains in unbelief the more honor she deserves for her perseverance. If, as a result of her faith, an unequally yoked wife is abandoned by her husband—the ultimate disaster for a wife—that woman should be regarded not as a failure but as one who has given her greatest possession for the love of Christ.

Too often, however, neither the church nor unequally yoked wives have that perspective. Often the woman who has the godliest husband is the most esteemed, while the wife of the town drunk is the most despised. A wife commonly receives admiration for being appreciated by her husband, while the woman who endures contempt from her unbelieving husband is viewed as one receiving recompense for her own shortcomings. This type of judgmentalism is grossly unjust.

Which wife daily sacrifices herself more—the one with the "perfect" Christian husband, or the one whose husband is imperfect? The one who appeases her husband by compromising her faith because she loves "the approval of men rather than the approval of God" (John 12:43), or the one who maintains her Christian testimony at the risk of disdain and disrespect from the one human being that she loves the most—her husband?

## The Weight Of The Cross

If a wife just behaves according to biblical mores, the church expects her unsaved husband to respond automatically with pleasure at her newfound faith. It is almost as if the church never read the words of Christ:

> "Do not think that I came to bring peace on the earth; I did not come to bring peace, but a sword. For I came to set a man against his father, and a daughter against her mother, and a daughter-in-law against her mother-in-law; and a man's enemies will be the members of his household"—Matthew 10:34-36.
>
> "Do you suppose that I came to grant peace on earth? I tell you, no, but rather division; for from now on five members in one household will be divided, three against two, and two against three."
>
> "If anyone comes to Me, and does not hate his own father and mother and wife and children and brothers and sisters, yes, and even his own life, he cannot be my disciple. Whoever does not carry his own cross and come after Me cannot be My disciple"—Luke 12:51-52; 14:26-27.

Does that sound like it should be easy to be an unequally yoked wife? Yet, a taint of gray has crept in upon the reputation of the unequally yoked wife, as if she deserves no more than the man she married. Since Christians are only supposed to marry other Christians, the wife of an unbeliever got what she deserved. Such is the common attitude in the church.

My own experience tells me that the overwhelming majority of unequally yoked wives did not marry unbelievers in rebellion against God. Most came to know Christ only after marrying another non-Christian. Often they were not raised in Christian households and had only a partial understanding of what it means to live a Christ-centered life. By the time they learned the "rules" about whom to marry, it was already too late.

What about those women who were already Christians and knew they should not marry an unbeliever? Do they deserve more condemnation than all the rest of us who have certainly disobeyed God on one point or another at some time in our Christian walk? Who among us pays a dearer price for our disobedience than the woman who must live with an unbelieving husband, perhaps for the rest of her natural life? We need not add further punishment with an unforgiving or condescending attitude toward these wives.

Instead of receiving compassion and support, wives of unbelievers are conditioned to expect no more than, at best, tolerant indifference from the church. How many churches have support groups for unequally yoked wives? How often are they ever mentioned from the pulpit, except to be reprimanded for what they are doing wrong?

At worst, they receive judgmental criticism from finger-pointing Christians who stand on the sidelines saying, "You ought to be a better wife; you'd have gotten your husband saved by now. Do this and listen to that if you want to be successful at getting him into the church. It's all up to you!"

Fearing to disobey what they think must be right, these guilt-ridden wives obediently jump to everyone's commands. Never once in all my years as the wife of an unbeliever did I think of putting my hands on my hips, stomping my foot, and shouting back to all those smug finger-pointers, "Great advice—*you* do it!"

No, I obeyed, failed, and hung my head like a whipped puppy. Thank God for the faithful few who stood with me unjudgmentally, or I may have felt completely worthless.

## Building Self-Esteem

I once read a trite story in a Christian women's magazine about how Susie Smart got saved and began to encounter persecution from her unsaved husband. Poor Susie didn't know what to do.

But then her neighbor, Mrs. Bold (whose husband also was unsaved), came over and advised Susie to insist that her husband attend church with her, throw out all his beer and cigarettes, and generally barge Christianity into his life for his own good.

Susie Smart, however, prayed to the Lord and decided that, rather than take Mrs. Bold's advice, she would just be a sweet, loving, submissive wife to her husband. And, *guess what?* Susie was so sweet and lovable that her husband became a Christian in just *two weeks!* Praise the Lord!

This story is a great example of the stereotypes many Christians have toward women whose husbands get saved versus those whose husbands remain in unbelief.

It wasn't until the last couple of years before my husband, Mark, became a Christian that I got comfortable enough with God to let down my defenses and receive a deeper revelation of His amazing unconditional love, acceptance, and even delight for me. Not until then could God heal my deepest inner wounds and begin to build in me a self-esteem that depended not on the approval of others but on His approval alone.

This is the kind of self-esteem I hope, in at least some small but miraculous way, to impart to each person reading these pages. I recognize, from my own sad experience, that there is a void in the institutional church in this area.

No segment of the church is in greater pain, in greater need, or in greater neglect than that large group of women whose husbands have not yet joined them in their faith. Unequally yoked Christian husbands experience many of the same difficulties, but I haven't mentioned them because I haven't experienced the battle from their side of the fence. I can't help but suspect, however, that their burdens must be a bit easier to bear in their role as the head of the house. I feel for them just the same.

There exists no lonelier plight for a married person to bear, other than the death of one's spouse, than that of being unequally yoked. I doubt, however, that even physical widowhood makes a woman feel as rejected and inadequate as does "spiritual widowhood"—the state of being married to one who is spiritually dead. The spiritual widow receives no flowers or sympathy cards. She simply grieves in silence for a union that never was.

## Refuge In Jesus

The times I needed the church the most were the times I felt the most unwanted. I remember on one rare and special occasion getting my husband's permission to attend an evening revival meeting with my sons. After the service, the boys begged to go to an "afterglow" meeting at a Christian couple's house. I was so pleased that they wanted to go that I smiled and said, "Oh, all right. Let's go!"

Later that evening I felt quite at home visiting with the couples who came, even though I was the only one there without a spouse. Then our host said loudly, "I get so sick of unequally yoked wives running around from one church meeting to another and begging everyone to pray for their unsaved husbands instead of staying home with their husbands where they belong.''

I sat through the rest of the meeting as numb with shock as if I had been slapped in the face. That man obviously felt that Christian fellowship was the private domain of Christian couples. Could he possibly imagine what it would be like never to spend time praying and sharing with other Christians? But what bothered me the most was that no one in the room seemed to object to his opinion. I managed to keep a straight face until I got out the door, but I cried all the way home.

After that experience I found it harder than ever to sit alone in church. I kept imagining that my solitary presence was an offense to the married couples there. So while the boys sat in their Sunday school classes, I spent many hours sitting in an empty room trying to cry out the hurt of feeling so rejected by what had been my greatest place of refuge—the church. There is some truth to the saying that the church is the only army that shoots its own wounded.

Thus I was presented with a turning point in my Christian life: I could choose to give up fighting the constant ego-crushing pressures of being an unequally yoked wife and drop out of the established church, as many woman have unfortunately done. Or I could receive God's tender healing, remembering that Jesus felt every one of my wounds as He hung on the cross. Then I could pick myself up, dust myself off, charge back into the church with all my might, and say, "Who do you people think you are, anyway? Jesus is my Lord, too!"

I'm glad I chose to do the latter. Eventually, I did change churches, and I found a different support group. But I thank the Lord for giving me the determination and guts to hang in there as a church-attending Christian. Why? Because many years later that is where my husband experienced new birth in Jesus Christ himself, forever changing his (and our) life.

God is faithful. When we offer Him our little sacrifices, He returns so much more to us. I offered Him my pride, time and again, as I walked into that church alone. God, in turn, gave me a husband to sit proudly beside in church today—a husband who is a joy and a delight and who appreciates unequally yoked wives. God finally penetrated that stony, guarded heart to give me a Christian husband who was well worth waiting for.

I am sure, my friend, that, as soon as possible, God will do the same for you. In the meantime, I pray that you will take comfort, encouragement, and hope from the words I have written in this book. Take freely of those words that may be helpful to you, and ignore freely any that are not. I certainly don't pretend to be an expert, just a fellow traveler who's been on that long, rough, rocky road.

Having finally reached that smooth place at the end of the road, I want to look back toward you who are still struggling along and say, "Keep on coming; don't give up! It's worth the effort! YOU'RE DOING JUST GREAT!"

# EPILOGUE

*"For we are a fragrance of Christ to God among those who are being saved and among those who are perishing"*—2 Corinthians 2:15.

Discouragement and depression hung about me like the overcast sky outside. Guilt and resentment wore at my peace of mind like the gusty winter winds heaving against the house. Tired of fighting negative thoughts, I sighed and turned away from the window.

"Father, I'm so weary of this constant battle of being married to a non-Christian. How can I ever win?"

I lay down on the sofa and tried to relax.

"Right now I am trying to think kind thoughts about my husband, but I just keep remembering his hostility and his cutting words. If only he would accept me as a Christian. And if only I could see him in a more loving way. . . ."

Then an idea came to me.

"Father, help me to see my husband as You do—through Your eyes. How *do* You see him, Lord? Please show me."

As I prayed with my eyes closed, I envisioned myself walking through a brightly colored, peaceful forest. I imagined the musty, leafy smells and the feeling of a gentle breeze wafting by. The sounds of birds calling and leaves rustling overhead filled me with a relaxing sense of God's presence.

Walking slowly through the forest, I was surprised to come upon a small clearing bursting with the most gorgeous flowers I had ever seen. They were lavender hyacinths, at least knee high. I knelt on the ground before them in awe. The blooms were large and vivid, their stems and leaves a lovely contrast of succulent lime green. But best of all was the aroma, like a thousand lilacs.

Carefully I reached out to touch one of the flowers. The Lord said, "Go ahead, enjoy them!" Bending down, I gathered armfuls of flowers to my face, bathing myself in their beauty and drinking deeply of their heavenly scent. What simple, peaceful joy those flowers gave.

But then I wondered, "Lord, I love these flowers. They are such a delight. But could You tell me, please, what does all this have to do with how You see my husband?"

The Lord's reply changed, from that moment on, the way I saw both my husband and myself.

"Notice how very beautiful these flowers are," He answered, tenderly, "how perfect, mature, and fragrant. They are indeed a delight. I want you to realize that these flowers are just the way I see you, My child."

I was amazed. Never had I seen myself as having such lovely qualities, especially in God's eyes. I had only seen myself as a struggling weakling, a flop, and a foolish child to God. Realizing that God saw none of those imperfections was incredible. Then the reason came to me clearly. When the Father looks at His children, He sees them through eyes of love; He sees every child of His through the atoning blood of Jesus, washed clean of every spot or wrinkle. All that remains for Him to see is the incredible beauty and potential that He designed into each of His creations.

Up until that time I had been taught that one should not think too highly of oneself. One should constantly be humbled by the awareness of one's own shortcomings. But that day I saw that the Lord doesn't look at His children from that negative perspective at all. Rather, He looks at us like a proud Father admiring His own children, seeing only the good, because we have been made "the righteousness of God" in Christ (2 Corinthians 5:21).

As I pondered that revelation I remembered my original question.

"Lord, I believe what You said about me—but what about my husband? How do You see him?"

149

He then directed my gaze to the edge of the cluster of flowers. "Look down there," He said. In the soil at the edge of the flowers was a pitiful seedling trying to pull itself up from the earth. With its head bent to the ground and its nose still in the dirt, the little plant looked puny and helpless beside those magnificent flowers. But a germ of life dwelt in that seedling: there was hope.

"That is how I see your husband," the Lord said gently.

"Oh, the poor little thing," I cried looking at the struggling green dollop. "What can I do to help it grow?"

"That," replied the Lord, "is My job—Mine alone. Your job is simply to be the beautiful flower I created you to be. Leave the rest to Me."

As the impact of those words hit me, waves of relief rolled through me. Feeling the heavy burden of guilt and responsibility for my husband's spiritual condition fall away, I understood the meaning of 1 Corinthians 3:6, "I planted, Apollos watered, but God was causing the growth." Yes, I could plant seeds, and others could water; but the ultimate responsibility for the results was up to God.

Until that day, I had only heard people telling me how I should act and what I should do to "get that husband saved," as if his salvation were my own *personal* responsibility. And all my frenzied efforts were not working. My husband still didn't believe, and I thought it was all my fault.

That is why the vision the Lord gave me that day changed my whole perspective and liberated me from guilt. At the same time, it freed me to grow in Christ without worrying about increasing the spiritual chasm between my husband and myself. I now understood that *God* was responsible for my husband's position in Christ, and that was no excuse for holding back my own growth. He wants us all to be as mature in Christ as possible. I would never be the same.

A couple of years after receiving this vision from the Lord, my husband became a Christian. Shortly after that I told him about the flowers and the seedling and how happy I was that he had grown under God's care. The next morning my husband woke up and said, "You wouldn't believe the dream I had last night. I dreamed about those flowers you told me about. I saw them, and I saw that little seedling, too. Then I saw the seedling tremble and start rising up out of the ground. It grew taller and taller until I started wondering what in the world it would become. Soon it was towering over the other flowers. Guess what it turned into."

I told him I couldn't imagine.

He beamed, "A sunflower!"

Indeed he has become a sunflower—and the sunshine in my life. Can God do the same for your husband? Of course! *Will* God do it? Why not? The Lord is no respector of persons.(See Acts 10:34.)

He has a perfect and loving plan for each and every person, including your husband.

You can relax in the comfort of trusting God to do His part, and, in the meantime, you are free to do your part. You are free to be the precious flower you have become in Christ. *Bloom!*

# ABOUT THE AUTHOR

Linda Davis is a registered nurse, real estate agent, speaker, and writer. A lifetime resident of the St. Louis area, she and her husband, Mark, are avid hot-air ballooning enthusiasts.

Married since the age of eighteen, Linda and Mark have two sons—Scot, a college student, and Todd, a senior in high school.

Linda's ministry gifts are in the areas of evangelism and encouraging others to a deeper relationship with Jesus Christ. She and her family are members of Grace World Outreach Church in St. Louis, Missouri.